T0157286

Facing Fears,
Quenching Flames

*Daily Devotional Guide
to Freedom
from Fear and Anger*

VIRGINIA GROUNDS

WESTBOW
PRESS
A DIVISION OF THOMAS NELSON

Copyright © 2013 Virginia Grounds.

All rights reserved. No part of this book may be used or reproduced by any means, graphic, electronic, or mechanical, including photocopying, recording, taping or by any information storage retrieval system without the written permission of the publisher except in the case of brief quotations embodied in critical articles and reviews.

WestBow Press books may be ordered through booksellers or by contacting:

WestBow Press
A Division of Thomas Nelson
1663 Liberty Drive
Bloomington, IN 47403
www.westbowpress.com
1-(866) 928-1240

Because of the dynamic nature of the Internet, any web addresses or links contained in this book may have changed since publication and may no longer be valid. The views expressed in this work are solely those of the author and do not necessarily reflect the views of the publisher, and the publisher hereby disclaims any responsibility for them.

Any people depicted in stock imagery provided by Thinkstock are models, and such images are being used for illustrative purposes only.

Certain stock imagery © Thinkstock.

ISBN: 978-1-4908-0233-6 (sc)
ISBN: 978-1-4908-0232-9 (e)

Library of Congress Control Number: 2013912961

Printed in the United States of America.

WestBow Press rev. date: 7/22/2013

Scripture taken from the New American Standard Bible®, Copyright © 1960, 1962, 1963, 1968, 1971, 1972, 1973, 1975, 1977, 1995 by The Lockman Foundation. Used by permission." (www.Lockman.org)

Scripture taken from the Holy Bible, New International Version®, NIV®. Copyright © 1973, 1978, 1984, 2011 by Biblica, Inc.™ Used by permission of Zondervan. All rights reserved worldwide. www.zondervan.com The "NIV" and "New International Version" are trademarks registered in the United States Patent and Trademark Office by Biblica, Inc.™ All rights reserved.

Scripture taken from the New King James Version. Copyright 1979, 1980, 1982 by Thomas Nelson, inc. Used by permission. All rights reserved.

Dedication

This book is dedicated to my husband because it is his compassion for hurting people and those in crisis that inspired these devotionals. Thank you Gene for your patience in the process of these experiences and for supporting me in what God leads me to do.

Table of Contents

Preface   xi

Introduction   xiii

Section One : Facing Your Fears   1

Take Courage   3

You Can Be Emotionally Strong   5

What Can Man Do To Me   8

Fear of Loss   10

Fear Leading To Depression   12

Fighting Back   16

Out of the Storm   19

Be Not Afraid   21

Shield of Faith   24

Childlike Faith   26

Casting Out Fear   28

What Now?   31

Rivers in the Desert   33

Declaration of Faith   36

Leaving the Past Behind   38

Tragedy to Triumph   41

When Fear Doesn't Win   43

The Better Choice 46

Compassion Motivates Action 49

Going Fishing 52

Fighting Tomorrows Battle 55

When Wounds Cut Deep 58

Calm the Raging Sea 61

A Fear That Calms 64

Section Two : Quenching the Flames of Anger 67

Beginning the Journey to Restoration Out of Anger 69

Turning Your Mad to Glad 73

Angry at God 76

Abundant in Mercy 79

Putting Things in Perspective 81

Does God Get Mad 83

Unmet Expectations 85

Words of Acceptance 88

When Anger Tries to Rule 90

Pulling Down Strongholds 93

Section Two : Quenching Flames - Breaking Down Anger 97

A = Anguish of Loss and Grief 99

N = Negative Input Impacts Future Response 101

G = Grief That Blames Others 103

E = Enemy of the Soul 106

R = Rejection Hurts 108

Section Two : Quenching Flames – Turning Anger Around 111

A = Acceptance and Adjustments in Life   113

N = New Way of Life   115

G = Grace Abundant and Free   117

E = Encouragement for the Soul   119

R = Redemptive Relationship   121

Section Two : Quenching Flames – Moving Beyond Anger 125

You Can Quench the Flames of Anger   127

Fatigue Fuels the Flame   130

When Crisis Interrupts...Power Intervenes   132

Drawn to the Well   135

Going Without Knowing   138

Preface

In serving alongside my husband in the ministry which God called him to many years ago, I have seen and spoken with many people who have experienced loss. I have seen the impact of negative emotions that have occurred as a result of grief. And, I have learned in my own life that there is really only one way to journey through grief, and that is by clinging to God and His word.

To grieve is to experience such intense sorrow and anguish that you feel as if it will never end. Along with grief comes an extensive list of emotions, one right on top of the other – fear, anger, pain, depression, to name a few. Grief can be caused by any type of loss ranging from the loss of a job to loss of a loved one. No one is immune to grief and the emotions that follow. All of us will experience it at some point in life.

How can we cope? How can we get past the emotions that drag us down? The focus of this book is on two of the most difficult emotions to overcome; fear and anger. My heart grieves for those who suffer loss and cannot get past these emotions to a state of peace and joy once again. God inspired the devotionals of this book to help hurting hearts overcome the impact of negative emotions that arise out of grief and loss. These devotionals are not your typical devotionals. They can be very convicting. Each one is a testimony and activity for you to work through on your own with prayer and Bible reading.

By picking up this book, you are beginning a journey to guide you through the emotions that follow your difficulty and loss. Section one is written to help you overcome the paralyzing fear that has resulted from whatever sorrow you have experienced. Section Two is a guide through overcoming anger and finding the freedom you long for.

My prayer for you as you begin this journey is that God will meet you every step of the way. In my life personally, I have found Him to be the greatest source of comfort in any need.

"My soul weeps because of grief; strengthen me according to Thy Word."
Psalm 119:28

Virginia Grounds

Introduction

Each time God places a topic for study on my heart, two things typically occur. The first is that I will have to experience firsthand what I am teaching or writing. As you can imagine, that is not always a fun thing to do as was the case of writing on fear and anger. I have been afraid, and I have been angry.

The second thing that occurs as I prepare to write is that God gives me a sensitivity and awareness of each time the word appears in Scripture. I love that! It is not something I plan, but rather something God does! He opens the eyes of my heart to see in what area He is leading me to teach or write. Now for those of you reading this who are seasoned Bible scholars, this is not new to you. But for the benefit of those who are new to the study of the Bible, it is exciting to see how God speaks to the hearts of those who are sharing the victories with them. I still get excited when I see God's hand at work, don't you?

And so, as I wrote on fear, much of what I shared was like a testimony of something I had already experienced and overcome. God has given me victory over fear. But much to my dismay, as I was writing on anger, its effects and consequences, I experienced it anew. I had an acute awareness of its presence in my life and the discussion of it in Scripture. And so, what is written on overcoming anger in this book is not simply words on a page. It is something experienced and the resulting inspiration God gave for overcoming fear and anger. These devotionals can be applied in the life of anyone experiencing negative emotions, and through this application process in your own life, you can overcome. You can be free! These are lessons we can all learn from.

I pray all who read it will approach it with an open heart and mind to what God wants to accomplish through it in each individual life. God can change your hurt and your heart if you really want Him to and are willing to take what He offers for overcoming the negative emotions of fear and anger. Often, we are so desperate to get past the pain of circumstances that we are willing to replace it with any Band-Aid fix. Instead of working toward God's healing with study, prayer and personal application, we allow the pain in our hearts to be replaced with fear and anger that can later turn to bitterness if we are not willing to do the work necessary to overcome.

In spite of whatever circumstance has filled you with negative emotions, peace can be the result of overcoming. You can experience the calm that follows a storm. And I praise God for the peace that is beyond understanding that can only come from Him. I pray God's peace will penetrate your heart and mind to replace any fear and angry residue left by pain so you can live life to the fullest according to His purpose for you.

I encourage you to read daily, but only one day's devotional at a time. Do not try to read them all in one sitting, but rather take each day in sequence, read the Scripture references, read the daily devotional and then pray for God to use what you have read to meet you at your point of need. Ask Him to show you your part in the process of victory over fear and anger. Come before Him with an open heart and a willing spirit to be healed. He will do the rest.

"Let us acknowledge the Lord. Let us press on to acknowledge Him. As surely as the sun rises, He will come to us like the winter rains, like the spring rains that water the earth."
Hosea 6:3

Section One

Facing Your Fears

Take Courage

"These things I have spoken to you, that in Me you may have peace. In the world you have tribulation, but take courage; I have overcome the world."
John 16:33

Scripture Reading: John 16:17-33

Fear can be an overwhelming thing. It can stem from people, things, or circumstances that have already occurred or that we fear will occur. It disrupts our lives and destroys our peace. How can you get past the fear that controls your emotions? How can you get beyond the past event that turned your world upside down and filled your heart with fear?

There is an answer to these questions. In the Bible, Jesus tells us there will be difficulty, or tribulation, in this world. And as long as we are alive and kicking, we know that trouble can come upon us in unexpected ways. Often that trouble leaves behind broken hearts, devastated lives, and fearful minds.

But in the same verse that tells you there will be trouble, there is given a first step toward getting beyond the fear, and that step is to take courage. Jesus said it to His disciples and it is still a first step for you today. "Take courage." Not only does He tell you how to move forward, but He gave a promise. He said, "I have overcome the world."

First, how do you "take" courage? Take is a verb. It means to put action to the thing spoken of – in this case courage. And so in

3

order to move beyond paralyzing fear, you must put action to courage. Grab hold of courage and make it yours! Take a stand – confidently make a commitment. "With God's help, I will be courageous. I will not allow fear to win. I will not allow the enemy to win."

Second, what does it mean to you personally that Jesus overcame the world? It means that if Christ is living in you, you have the power within you to overcome whatever this world throws your way! God can, and will, be in control of our emotions if we will let Him. When Jesus said "I have overcome the world", that statement was not only a promise but a fact. He has overcome; therefore, you can! Pray and ask Him to help you overcome your fears. Ask Him to be in control of your emotions and to strengthen your mind with courage.

Today's Prayer: *Lord, I ask that you will be in control of my emotions today. Thank you that you have overcome the world including the fears that come from people and circumstances in my life. Fill my heart with courage that I may take the first step out of fear and into a life strengthened to move forward trusting You. Amen*

You Can Be Emotionally Strong

"...not by might nor by power, but by my Spirit says the Lord."
Zechariah 4:6

Scripture Reading: John 14:25-27

Uncontrolled emotions can become so overwhelming that we stumble and fall in the midst of the challenging circumstances we face. Fear, worry, anger and negative thinking can result from uncontrolled emotions.

At a time of overwhelming challenges in my own life, a very wise man said to me, "Virginia, you say you are trusting God with this situation, but have you ever asked Him to specifically be in control of your emotions." At that time in my life, I had not thought to pray in that way. And so I began to ask God's Holy Spirit to be in control of my emotions for each day. It became part of my daily morning prayers until I began to sense a difference in my stress level. I learned that God truly does have the power to rule in our hearts in such a way that we are impacted by His peace.

It has been many years since I received those words of wisdom, but even now in difficult circumstances when I feel my emotions controlling me, I turn them over to God. He has never failed to calm me, fill my heart with peace and enable me to endure and press on.

God promises that His Spirit will be in the battles of life with us; and let's face it, at times our emotions are at war within us! The words of Jesus have given me the wonderful assurance of His Spirit in my life to help me, teach me and fill me with peace so that I will not be afraid in times of trouble.

> *"But the Helper, the Holy Spirit, whom the Father will send in My name, He will teach you all things, and bring to your remembrance all that I said to you. Peace I leave with you; My peace I give to you; not as the world gives, do I give to you. Let not your heart be troubled, nor let it be fearful."*
> John 14:26-27

Jesus sent His Spirit to live within us. And it is by His Spirit that we can be strengthened emotionally to walk through whatever circumstances we encounter and beyond. Believers can be encouraged by His presence in our lives to control that which overwhelms us. The weapon He uses to win the war is His sword. What is His sword? It is the word of God.

> *"...and the sword of the Spirit, which is the word of God."*
> Ephesians 6:17

And so as we read the Bible and pray He will, by the power of His Holy Spirit, conquer your emotions with peace. If you want to win the war raging inside you, read the Bible daily and pray that God will be in control of your emotions.

Today's Prayer: *Lord, I am a vessel that has been weakened by circumstances outside my body which have fractured the state of those things inside my body. My heart and mind are wounded to the point that I am an emotional wreck. Today, I am turning the control of my emotions over to you. Please Lord be in control of my emotions in such a way as to fill my heart with*

peace. Strengthen my mind to be able to overcome fear, anger or whatever emotion is trying to keep me captive. I ask your Holy Spirit to rule in every aspect of my life to bring healing to my wounded spirit. Amen

What Can Man Do To Me

"I called on the LORD in distress; the LORD answered m...The LORD is on my side; I will not fear. What can man do to me?"
Psalm 118:5a, 6

Scripture reading: Psalm 118

In writing the Psalm, King David poured out his heart to the Lord. There is so much about overcoming fear we can learn from him. He was constantly being attacked from all sides; both personally and professionally as King. But David had learned the key to personal peace and that was to look, not only to the identity of the Lord, but to remind himself of God's actions for him and His mercy which endures forever.

When he cried out to the Lord in his distress, God answered. When he was pushed violently so he would fall, God helped him. When he thought he would die from the consequences of sin, God saved him from death. And so, David committed his life to exalting God and giving praise to His holy Name.

A client of our ministry once told us that when she was being attacked in a parking lot, she cried out to the Lord and He gave her the supernatural strength to hit the offender with a gallon of milk. When we read about God's actions in the Bible, we have a tendency to look at them as "then". But this women's story proves that what God did in the days of the Bible, He will do today in the lives of those who cry out to Him.

David said the enemy had pushed him violently so he would fall, but the LORD helped him. That is what happened to this woman. She was pushed violently so she would fall, but God helped her. You see, as He was with David, He will be with you. God is on your side! And with God on your side, there is hope, help and healing. His mercy endures forever. Cry out to Him in your distress and He will answer. Give Him praise for who He is and what He has done. Claim His promise of hope for your life today.

Today's Prayer: *Holy Father, I give you praise today for your saving grace and for your mercies which are forever. Thank you for the promise I find in your word that you will answer when I cry out to you. I'm crying out to you Lord for help in becoming emotionally strong that I will not fall when pushed by the words or actions of those who seek to bring me down. Thank you for your strength, help and healing. In the power of Jesus Name I pray, Amen.*

Fear of Loss

*"Fear and a snare have come upon us, desolation and
destruction. My eyes overflow with rivers of water for
the destruction of the daughter of my people."*
Lamentations 3:47-48

Scripture Reading: Lamentations 3:46-60, Romans
8:26-27

In the book of Lamentations, the prophet Jeremiah grieved over
Israel and the loss of life there from the enemies of the land. He
grieved as well for the loss of faith of the people. Fear had become
the snare of defeat for the hearts of the people. Jeremiah cried out
to the Lord for justice. He literally cried tears of grief for those
who died and for those who were suffering. As he prayed to the
Lord, He acknowledged in verse 56 that God heard his voice and
was near to him. Then God said three very important words that
are still words of hope for you today. "Do not fear".

There are occasions in life when things are so difficult, all you
can do is cry. In fact, the words of Jeremiah indicated that he was
sobbing all the time and his soul was hurting because of loss. I
remember a time in my life when the realization of loss became
so great that I couldn't stop crying. At times, it seemed I was
crying for no reason at all. I couldn't identify the source of the
tears. The only way I was able to get beyond those days was to do
as Jeremiah did – cry out to the Lord. I love what verse 58 in the
scripture reading above says. *"O Lord, you have pleaded the case
for my soul; you have redeemed my life."*

In days of facing grief and loss, there is a promise from God's word that will see you through. He has pleaded your case! He had redeemed you. That means He has bought you back from the enemy of the soul. And because He has, you can live with the promise of His intercession for you. You can see that more clearly for believers today in Romans 8:26. *"Likewise the Spirit also helps in our weaknesses. For we do not know what we should pray for as we ought, but the Spirit Himself makes intercession for us with groaning which cannot be uttered."*

God has sent His Holy Spirit to intercede on your behalf with groaning too deep for words during those days when you don't know how, or simply cannot pray as you should because you are weakened by grief and loss. When God's Holy Spirit prays for you, your troubled heart will begin to heal. Ask Him to intercede on your behalf.

Today's Prayer: *Father, I thank you for redeeming me from the enemy of my soul. But now, in my fear of loss and grief, I am so emotional that I can't even think straight. And so, I ask that your Holy Spirit intercede on my behalf that I may be healed from my fears and overpowering emotions of loss. I am claiming your promise of hearing my voice. Thank you I pray, Amen.*

Fear Leading To Depression

*"But he himself went a day's journey into the wilderness,
and came and sat down under a broom tree. And he
prayed that he might die and said, "It is enough! Now,
Lord, take my life for I am no better than my fathers."*
I Kings 19:4

Scripture Reading I Kings 19:1-18

There are times in life when we all feel sad or experience grief, but depression is a deeper level of emotional turmoil that affects many people in many ways. According to research, nearly one person in five will experience levels of depression. It causes people to miss more work than diabetes or heart disease.

It can be caused by a variety of factors including stress, fear, loneliness, guilt and anger; and is not new to our generation. The Bible tells of people who experienced depression for various reasons. In Psalm 38, David described depression from unconfessed sin. God used grief and depression to get Nehemiah's attention to do His work according to Nehemiah 1:4; in the book of Job, he experienced financial, personal, and relational losses that led him to curse the day he was born.

But Elijah is a man, a prophet of God, who experienced fear that led him to run and experience depression. You read about this in the scripture reading referenced above.

Depression has a way of draining energy, twisting values, and assaulting faith. This story of Elijah is an example of how depression can strike anyone, even godly leaders. Elijah was a prophet of God who had just experienced a spiritual victory. He exhibited great courage in the face of evil, confronting kings and false prophets. Yet when Queen Jezebel threatened to kill him, he ran for his life and lapsed into a deep depression. When Jezebel threatened him, he reacted in fear.

Fear is prevalent in many kinds of depression – anxiety and depression coexist in seventy percent of those diagnosed with depression. Proverbs 12:25 says *"Anxiety in the heart of man causes depression, but a good word makes it glad."*

Fear drove him to run which led to depression. Depression can paralyze us emotionally causing us to HALT in our tracks. Look at how this emotional assault is exhibited in him.

> **H** – Hungry – verses 4-5 – He stopped eating

> **A** – Angry – He was mad at God for not caring about him and prayed he would die.

> **L** – Lonely – He left his servant and traveled alone.

> **T** – Tired – He collapsed into sleep.

But we see hope for recovery in God's response to Elijah's emotional downward spiral. He counteracted the HALT syndrome with hope in Elijah's life at every level.

First, God provided his physical needs of the moment. An angel touched him and said arise and eat. When he looked, there by his head was a cake baked and a jar of water. Food and water are necessary ingredients to sustain the body when it is depleted from stress, grief, exhaustion or fear.

Next, God provided his emotional needs with the presence of the angel. Elijah was not as alone as he thought he was. Two times he was encouraged to regain his strength by eating, drinking and resting and he went in the strength of that food forty days and nights as far as Horeb, the mountain of God.

God provided his spiritual needs through a still small voice. (19:12-18)

God brought Elijah out of the HALT syndrome which enabled him to listen to God and obey what he said.

This story reminds us of the importance of having a real and personal relationship with God. When we are depressed, we may often feel like running away from our problems like Elijah. But as tempting as it may be, we must avoid isolating ourselves and giving up hope. And though he felt hopeless, Elijah was willing to accept God's help. He recognized God's voice and was strengthened and encouraged. Then he was able to return to his life and mission with a new ability to cope and a new hope for the future.

God responded with mercy to Elijah. He did not condemn him for his condition – something that many depressed Christians expect from God. Instead, God provided what he needed and then encouraged him to "go" and continue his work.

What we learn from this are several principals for help.

Don't give up on life, don't give in to emotional turmoil; but continue on the path where God has placed you. Listen to the still small voice of God and do what He says. Through all of what Elijah experienced, he learned that God would never forsake him or leave him. Out of His love and mercy, God showed him a way out of despair.

And just as he has shown Elijah, He will surely show you as He works quietly day by day in the hearts and souls of His people to provide HOPE for the future.

H – Help and healing (food, water, rest; verses 5-7)

O – Opportunity (go, verse 15)

P – Plan for your life (do, verses 15-18)

E – Encouragement (still small voice, presence of God, conversation with God, verse 12)

Let us encourage one another with the hope that is within us as we follow God's plan of taking every opportunity to do His work. Rest when we need to, eat when we are hungry, drink when thirsty so we will be strengthened to press on and to conquer the emotions leading to depression.

Today's Prayer: *Lord, my life is in your hands. Thank you for the hope I have because of your love and mercy. Help me to rest when I need to, eat and drink when necessary in order to strengthen my body against depression. In Jesus name, Amen.*

Fighting Back

*"I hate the work of those who fall away. It
shall not fasten its grip on me."*
Psalm 101:3

The thing about difficult circumstances is that they are so... well, wearing! One or two – maybe even three difficulties at the same time can be dealt with, but when crisis upon crisis occurs like dominos falling, your body and mind do not have time to recover before the next crisis hits. The impact of stress on the body and mind leave you depleted of internal resources to cope, and you find yourself in despair. What can you do when you reach this level of physical, emotional, and spiritual weariness?

There was a time years ago when I found myself in this state. Loss of income, death of loved ones, shoulder surgery, loss of friendships and other disappointments had taken their toll on my mind and body. I felt I was so buried in despair I could never dig my way out. But I refused to give in to the pressure to give up and walk away from God. A few years prior to that time, I watched as people I knew and loved turned their back on God, and what they knew to be the right thing, in order to do what was right in their own eyes. I knew I did not want to do the same thing. Deep down, I knew that turning away from God was not the answer even though at times I felt forsaken.

When I sat down to pray, the words would not come. I found myself crying to God saying "O God, please do not let me go. Even

16

though I have lost my grip on you, please do not let me go but keep me in the palm of your hand."

As I cried out to Him, I found Psalm 101:3. The words of this verse were like a surge of energy to my soul. *"I hate the work of those who fall away. It shall not fasten its grip on me."*

This verse became my commitment to the Lord during a difficult time. My commitment was that I would not allow life's troubles to fasten their grip on me forcing me away from God and my faith. I felt I was losing my grip, but I also knew of God's promise to never leave me nor forsake me. I clung to that promise even during the times when I questioned it.

God heard the cry of a wounded heart, a defeated mind, and a weary body. He brought me out of the miry clay, set my feet upon the Rock, and filled my mouth with praise to My God. Psalm 40:1-3. He healed my broken heart, and has used the difficulties of my past to soften me in response to the pain of others. He has forced me, through my own suffering, to be more flexible, understanding, and patient when faced with the suffering of others. Broken relationships in my life have been mended because I am more forgiving having been taught forgiveness while in the fires of tribulation. I didn't like having to go through everything I went through, but God was with me through it all and has not wasted the experiences but is using them for His glory.

When trials come, it is so important to cling to what we know to be true about God because His promises are true! The answer to the question in the first paragraph is; fight back. Don't give up… don't give in, but fight back with Truth and eyes toward Heaven!

- He will hear when you cry out to Him – Psalm 40:1

- He will comfort you – Isaiah 66:13

- He will be a refuge and source of strength to you – Psalm 46:1

- He will rescue you from despair – Psalm 42:11

- He will fill your heart with peace – Phil. 4:7

- He will fill your mouth with praise – Psalm 63:3

Thanks be to God that as I place my trust in Him no matter what life brings my way, I am blessed!

Today's Prayer: *Lord, thank you that we have the promise from you that as we place our trust in you, we are blessed. Help me to trust you more when difficulty surrounds me. In Jesus Name, Amen.*

Out of the Storm

*I saw... "Like the appearance of a rainbow in the clouds on
a rainy day, so was the radiance around Him. This was the
appearance of the likeness of the glory of the LORD. When I
saw it, I fell facedown, and I heard the voice of One speaking."*
Ezekiel 1:28

Scripture Reading: Ezekiel 1:4-28

Life is full of storms. I remember the storms that came suddenly in
the West Texas town where I grew up. Dark clouds and lightening
would fill the sky with predictions of tornados. My mother was
raised in Chicago and not accustomed to the West Texas weather.
She would wait as long as she could stand it, but sure enough, we
would be taken to the storm cellar. It is interesting that as I look back,
I don't remember being afraid. I felt secure in knowing that in the
storm, we would be safe because she would see to it that we were.

In the Bible, Ezekiel saw a storm coming. The way it is described
sounds like those West Texas storms. It was a, *"windstorm from the
North, an immense cloud with flashing lightning and surrounded
by brilliant light and filled with fire."* But this storm was different.
It held within it a vision of the Lord for Ezekiel to see. God was
in the storm!

Often, as we face our own personal storms: health, finances,
relationships, job security and other situations, we feel alone in
the middle of it. Things may seem hopeless. But God has promised
never to leave us or forsake us. He is with you in the middle of the
storms you face.

Surrounded by what seemed hopeless, Ezekiel saw the storm coming, but out of the midst of it, he heard the voice of God and saw His glory as a rainbow. What is God saying to you in the middle of your storm? Look for the promise of His rainbow which is a reflection of His glory, mercy and love. Listen for His voice and look toward the heavens for hope when things seem hopeless. Seek and you will find the Lord.

Today's Prayer: *Father, it is so comforting to know that when storm clouds roll in and fear takes hold like flashes of lightening, you are there in the midst of my despair with me. Open my ears to your voice and my eyes to clearly see you in my life. In Jesus name, Amen*

Be Not Afraid

"You are from God, little children, and have overcome them,
because greater is He who is in you than he who is in the world."
I John 4:4

Scripture Reading: First John 4

Life in this world is filled with uncertainty. No one knows what tomorrow will bring, and security is something very important to us. We all want to have secure lives and futures. We want to know that we are loved. If we have a career, we want to know we will always be appreciated in our work. If we have children, we want to know that the future holds wonderful promises for them. We want to know that our home will stand no matter what. And so when something happens in our lives to shake the foundation that we thought was solid, we become afraid for the future.

I can tell you from experience that fear, is not only paralyzing, but destructive. As a young adult in my early twenties, both my parents died within a few years of each other. And as a young, single mom, I had depended upon my mother for advice and direction. In the years following her death, I experienced so much fear that it controlled my life to the point of almost destroying it and every relationship I had. The foundation of my existence had been shaken and as I looked to the future, I was paralyzed with questions, doubts and fear.

It wasn't until years later after I became a Christian and began to study the Bible that I was able to overcome the fear of not knowing what the future would bring. The first verse God used to help me was First Timothy 1:7. *"For God has not given us a spirit of timidity, but power and love and discipline."* The Greek definition for the word timidity is fear and the word for discipline is sound mind. And so I began to pray and claim this verse for my life every day until I began to see a difference in my emotions. I would pray, 'Lord, thank you that you have not given me a spirit of fear, therefore I know that fear is not of you. But You have given me power, love and a sound mind, and I pray your power will overpower my fears and push them out of my heart and mind.'

Following the realization that paralyzing fear is not from God, there had to be a change in my heart and mind regarding trust. God does not want fear to destroy our lives and He gives us the power and sound mind to overcome it. And so, the next step is to trust Him to do in the present what He has already done in the past and to rest in the knowledge of His love. God's love is perfect and there is no fear in His love according to First John 4:18. In fact the verse tells us that His perfect love casts out fear! We can trust Him to remove the fear from our hearts as we trust Him and ask Him to do it. We can be secure in the future as we give our fears to Him and thank Him for casting them out of our lives. We can overcome! Why? *"You are from God, little children, and have overcome them; because greater is He who is in you than he who is in the world."* (Emphasis mine) First John 4:4. This became a life verse for me and I still pray it and claim it in those times when circumstances begin to overwhelm me.

And finally, we receive the help we need to get past our fears by listening to the words of Jesus as He spoke to the disciples in John 14:27. *"Peace I leave with you; My peace I give to you; not as the world gives, do I give to you. Let not your heart be troubled, nor let it be fearful."* As we recognize that fear is not from God, as we ask Him to overpower it and trust Him to do it; Jesus fills our hearts with His peace. Not the kind the world offers, but a deep abiding rest from our fears that comes from believing in Him and believing Him.

Whatever difficult circumstances you face today that are causing you paralyzing fear, Jesus says; *"Let not your heart be troubled; believe in God, believe also in Me."* John 14:1. May you experience His peace today as you overcome your fears by His power.

Today's Prayer: *Father, I thank you that greater is He who lives in me than the fears this world has to offer. Today, I ask that your presence be made evident in my life to defeat my fears and experience your peace. In Jesus name, Amen.*

Shield of Faith

"Put on the whole armor of God that you may be
able to stand against the wiles of the devil."
Ephesians 6:11

In the days of the Bible when warriors went into battle, they wore armor and took shields with them to protect themselves from the weapons of the enemy. How they left from the battle was dependent upon skill, use of their weapons and protective armor. In up close combat, it was the lifting of the shield that served as a source of protection. Lifting the shield became an automatic reaction to the immediate threat in front of them.

I've never been a soldier, but am sure soldiers experience fear at times before or during the battle. And yet, they charge in because that is what they are commanded to do and must do in order to win and to live. Withdrawal is not an option when the enemy is charging forward toward them. And so, their response to fear is obedience and action.

In a way, paralyzing fear becomes an emotional enemy and battle we must face head on if we are to win over it. How do you respond to fear? Do you withdraw and live in it day by day, or do you equip yourself to forge ahead facing your fears in order to win over them.

The Scripture reading for today gives the believer instruction for how to face the battles in our lives that must be fought. Your most important armor against them is to be strong in the Lord and in the power of His might. God gives you strength and power to face your fears. These verses tell us to put on God's armor of truth, righteousness, the gospel of peace, shield of faith, salvation and the Holy Spirit. Then pray. Put on the armor, lift up the shield, pray and enter the battle to overcome your fears.

God will be with you to enable you to stand against the fiery darts of the enemy. And the enemy of this world shoots darts at any area of our lives where he senses weakness. If fear is evident in our lives, Satan uses that weakness to direct our focus to defeat.

The fiery darts of Biblical days were arrows covered with tar and set on fire. They were then shot into the bodies of soldiers. Verse 16 instructs us to *lift* the shield of faith. It is faith in Christ that produces a shielding effect that extinguishes Satan's flaming attempts to destroy our emotions.

Lift your shield of faith so you may have victory over the fears that are controlling your emotions. Renew your trust in God for strength and power to overcome.

Today's Prayer: *Heavenly Father, I lift up my shield of faith in you today for protection from the fiery darts of the enemy. O Lord, I can only imagine the pain from burning tar thrust into a body, but I know the pain from emotional trauma that burns within. And so, I thank you for your armor of protection by your Holy Spirit to guard me from pain and fear. Protect and heal me O Lord, I pray. In Jesus name, Amen.*

Childlike Faith

"When I am afraid, I will put my trust in God."
Psalm 56:3

Years ago I was listening to a radio talk show and heard a young mother talking about a life-threatening surgery her three year old son was scheduled to have. She knew the moment would come when she would not be allowed to go into the operating room with him and wanted to prepare him for that moment. And so, she taught her young son verses from the Bible to help him in the moments of their separation. She prayed he would not be afraid and would be protected.

When it was all over and he was able to talk again, she asked him if he had been afraid. In his sweet three year old voice he said, "No mommy. You told me to say 'when I am afraid, I will trust in God', and that is what I did.

To have such childlike faith in those moments of our fear is a heart that is calm in the face of it. That mother had taught her son the words of Psalm 56:3. Those same words are ours to claim as well, *"When I am afraid, I will put my trust in Thee."*

But there is much more to this passage of scripture. It describes a time in the life of the writer when he was being attacked and fighting against evil. But David recognized that every tear he had shed was not only known by God, but captured in a bottle. Out of David's fear came sorrow, and God knew it very well and made note of it.

As a loving Heavenly Father, He, like that young mother, teaches us not to fear as we face the uncertainties of life. No matter where we have been, no matter what sorrows, God knows and He cares for you. Put your trust in Him.

Today's Prayer: *Lord, it is beyond me to understand how you can know every tear I shed and hold it in a bottle. And yet, your word says it is true. And so, I trust you in the circumstances of life that cause me to fear. "When I am afraid, I will trust in Thee". You are amazing... Amen*

Casting Out Fear

"There is no fear in love; but perfect love casts
out fear, because fear involves punishment, and
the one who fears is not perfected in love."
I John 4:18

Scripture Reading: I John 4:11-19

Fear of a person to the point of being paralyzed is a miserable experience. It can stop you from being the person God intended you to be. It can prevent you from experiencing joy and a sense of fulfillment. And, it can damage all other relationships in your life. Fear is like a brick wall standing between you and life as it was intended.

But God has a promise for those experiencing paralyzing fear. He promises that His perfect love will get rid of it. Perfect love is that which is not found wanting. It is fully satisfied. It is the love which accomplishes its goal – in this case, to cast out fear. In First I John 4:15-19, God gives a guide to help you get rid of fear in your life.

First, verse 15 says to confess Jesus as the son of God and abide, that is live, in Him. His promise is to live in you as you abide in Him.

Second, believe that God loves you because God is love.

Next, accept His love. There are moments in life when that is not as easy to do as it sounds. Accepting that God loves you, when you have been pressed down by real people causing you to feel unloved, is difficult. But God's love is perfect and is with you so that you can be as He is in this world – perfected in His love. You are able to love Him and accept His love because He first loved you. Is that awesome or what? God loves you and loved you first long before you had any expectation of love from others and long before you knew Him or loved Him!

Finally, in verse 18 is the promise of God that there is no fear in His love. Why? Because His love is perfect and perfect love casts out fear! That is His wonderful promise for you today.

The verse goes on to explain that fear involves punishment. In other words, you may be afraid because of some past event of pain in your life. Therefore, each time the pain surfaces, you become fearful that something similar will happen again.

And so, the verse continues *"the one who fears is not perfected in love"*. That sounds harsh, but it simply means that you may be allowing fear to conquer the power of God's love in your life. We all do so at some point, and by so doing, we are allowing fear to win! In order to live out God's promise to get rid of the fear is going to take some action on our part. We need to set our hearts and minds on Him accepting that His love is more powerful than anything this world can throw our way. Confess, believe, and accept the perfection of love that is ours through Jesus Christ. And remember; His is a love that is not found wanting and finishes what it begins. When He promises that His perfect love will get rid of your fear, He will complete that promise in you. Ask Him to do so today.

Today's Prayer: *Lord, I confess that I am a fearful person because of past experiences of pain and punishment. But I confess and*

acknowledge that Jesus is your Son in whom I will abide in order to experience your perfect love. I believe that you love me and accept your love and the fact that there is no place in your love for fear. Thank you for casting fear from my heart and mind. Fill me now with thoughts of you to replace the thoughts of the past which have caused me to fear. Invade my heart, mind and life with your power to overcome my fears. I thank you and praise you in Jesus name, Amen.

What Now?

"As one whom his mother comforts, so I will comfort you..."
Isaiah 66:13a

The pain of loss often seems more than we can bear

The sorrow and mourning are evident and like garments we wear.

But know that pain is but a journey through grief, tears and sorrow;

A journey through the valley of loss toward healing

And a hopeful tomorrow.

So look toward the future even though the journey takes time

Keep walking through the valley

And try to see each step through God's eyes.

Because God knows your sorrow, He knows your pain.

He knows your life will never be the same.

But His love is everlasting, His mercies are poured on you.

He is your source of comfort, and He will see you through.

> *"Blessed be the God and Father of our Lord Jesus Christ,*
> *the Father of mercies and God of all comfort, who*
> *comforts us in all our tribulation that we may be able to*
> *comfort those who are in any trouble, with the comfort*
> *with which we ourselves are comforted by God."*
> Second Corinthians 1:3-4

Today's Prayer: *Lord, you are my comforter. I know this pain I am experiencing from loss is not a surprise to you but I pray for relief. Help me now. Amen*

Rivers in the Desert

"I will make a roadway in the wilderness, rivers in the desert."
Isaiah 43:19b

Scripture Reading: Exodus 2 and 3

Let's face it. There are seasons in life that are simply dry. They just are! We don't plan for there to be drought in our spirit or circumstances, and especially not in our provisions; but desert times do occur in spite of our expectations.

How do we survive the wilderness experiences of life? The key to survival is being prepared in a way that sustains you as you journey through the lonely desert places. God promised to make a way in the wilderness - a way to nourish our dry and weary souls as we seek Him, trust Him, and believe Him. He is your oasis in the desert! He will never take you to a place where He does not plan to go with you on the journey. In fact, it may surprise you to learn that if you find yourself in a desert experience, God has prepared you, not only to be there, but to survive it. He has gone before you to the end result. He has equipped you in advance for what will take place there.

If you have ever been on a camping trip, moved from one city to another or taken any journey, you know how much planning must go into the packing and preparation for departure. Of course if you are "in charge," others with you just assume that all their meals, clothing and gear just jumped in the vehicle of their own accord in order to be there for them when they arrived. The point is, someone prepared in advance for what would take place on the journey.

We see God's advance preparation in the life of Moses from Exodus Chapters two and three. God called him from a task of familiarity to prepare him for a desert experience that would take him far beyond his comfort zone. Moses was leading the flock of his father-in-law. Leading indicates moving forward. So, he was taking them somewhere. Scripture says "*...he led the flock to the west side of the wilderness (desert) and came to Horeb, the mountain of God.*"

Moses left for work that day to take care of his responsibilities of feeding and watering the flock. Even in the most forbidding environment, a little water will create a refuge, and plants, animals, and humans will flock to it. A spot like this is called an oasis. In the desert, oases are fertile spots where nomads' caravans stopped to replenish their water supply.

Perhaps Moses was searching for an oasis in the desert, a place where he could rest from the heat while the flock was satisfied. He was alone with just his responsibility, but he did not realize that God was leading him to an encounter with Him that would change his life for the rest of his days.

Being alone with only our responsibilities to keep us company can cause us to be lonely and discouraged. You may be a single parent carrying the responsibility for your children alone. You may be a corporate executive with an entire staff looking to you for decisions. You may be someone who has lost your loved one or been victimized in some way. All of these circumstances can dry out your spirit and cause you to feel you are in a lonely desert. It is during this time that you need an oasis ... cool refreshment from the suffering in your life.

Look again at the scripture verse for today at the beginning of this reading. Just as God led Moses to water, He promises for you rivers in your desert. Trust Him to lead you there and then encounter the Living Water who is Jesus Christ. He will change your life forever. He brings refreshment for your dry spirit so you can live in the oasis of His presence for healing, rest and a fruitful life.

"...Jesus stood and cried out saying, "if anyone thirsts, let him come to Me and drink. He who believes in Me, as the Scripture has said, out of his heart will flow rivers of living water."
John 7:37-38

Today's Prayer: *Precious Jesus, I am so thankful to know you and to experience the fullness of joy that springs from you the Living Water of a soul that was once dry. Thank you for rescuing me from the dryness and loneliness of the desert. Amen.*

Declaration of Faith

"The LORD is my light and my salvation, whom shall I fear?
The LORD is the strength of my life, of whom shall I be afraid?
Psalm 27:1

Scripture Reading: Psalm 27

Whom shall I fear? The Psalmist asks the question of himself with confidence that he need not fear. Why? Because he has identified who the LORD is in his life. He declared his faith in the LORD as his light, salvation and strength, and with God by his side, there is no one to fear. He is so confident in fact, that in verse three, he stated that even though war may rise against him, and an army may surround him, he was confident that his heart would not fear.

Do you long for that kind of confidence? Does your heart fear a person or circumstance that seems much bigger than you can cope with? One of the controlling aspects of fear is that it promotes a lifestyle that is dominated by what you are trying to avoid. Avoiding the person or circumstance you are afraid of is not the answer for overcoming the fear of them or the circumstance. It only prolongs the fear. But, I know from personal experience that fear can be defeated. We find the proof of that in God's word.

We learn from Psalm 27:1-3 that the Psalmist gained confidence by declaring his faith in the identification of who God is in his life. God had been to him a light to dispel the darkness. When negative emotions control your thoughts, you can often feel you are living in darkness. But God will be a light within your heart as you know Him and believe in Him. That is the salvation the Psalmist describes – to know and believe God, trusting Him with your life. Next, the LORD is identified as the strength of his life. But in Psalm 28:7, another identity is added to His strength. It says, *"The LORD is my strength and my shield …"*. His heart trusted in Him and he was helped.

On previous days, you have already read about the shield of faith. Our help comes from lifting our shield which is faith. You may ask, "How do I lift up a shield that I cannot see?" I believe the answer is found in these verses in the Psalms. God is your shield. Your faith in Him is declared as you lift up His Holy Name for praise and by identifying who He is in your life. Lifting a shield of faith for protection from our fears is a matter of knowing who God is, believing His word is true and trusting our lives to Him. After identifying the LORD as his strength and shield, the Psalmist stated that his heart trusted in Him, and he was helped.

And so, from the Psalmist we learn some steps to overcome fear and to be filled with the confidence of help:

- Declare faith in God

- Identify who He is in your life

- Trust in Him

Today's Prayer: *Lord, I trust in you today to deliver me from those emotions that are preventing me from being who you desire me to be. I know that you are my light, my salvation, my strength and my shield. I lift up your holy Name for praise today and have confidence that you are a shield before me protecting me from whatever I fear may harm me, and therefore, I rejoice in you. I thank you Jesus. Amen.*

Leaving the Past Behind

"And Moses said to the people, 'do not be afraid.
Stand still and see the salvation of the LORD, which
He will accomplish for you today... The LORD will
fight for you, and you shall hold your peace."
Exodus 14:13a-c, 14

Scripture Reading: Exodus 13:21- 14:31

On a response to help victims following tornadoes that swept through Moore, Oklahoma, my husband became trapped between five *new* tornadoes; three in front of him and two behind. It was late afternoon but the skies were black. He drove to the side of the road just as lights all over town lost power. He was engulfed in darkness. He admitted it was the most afraid he had ever been in his life! He could feel the tug on his vehicle as the back end was continuously lifted up and down. He cried out to Jesus and was spared from harm.

This incident reminded me of Moses and the Israelites as they ran from danger. What would you do if you were traveling on a journey that was taking you into the unknown, and you became trapped between two dangers?

The story of Moses and the Israelites when they were trapped between two dangers is a story with a miraculous ending of epic proportions - the parting of the Red Sea. And yet, you can read in Exodus 14 about the fear of the people because they looked behind them and saw a vicious foe, but in front of them a raging sea. They were afraid to move forward. Though they cried out to the Lord, they had no confidence He could help. Quickly forgetting the pain of the past, they bitterly accused Moses of deceiving them by leading them into the desert to die. They panicked and had a lack of confidence in his leadership. It was fear that prevented them from trusting the Lord for deliverance from danger. They wanted to go back!

Moses recognized that fear was distorting their memories and arousing their passions against him. He sought to reassure them that the Lord would deliver them by fighting for them as they remained firm in confidence. But as they came to their greatest moment of deliverance, the people of God were full of distrust and fear. When confronted with trouble, they looked back to Egypt, but God said "go forward".

God's intent was to save the people from harm. He told the people to go forward but He went behind. *"And the angel of God who had been going before the camp of Israel moved and went behind them, and the pillar of cloud moved from before them and stood behind them."* Verse 15.

The next verse indicates that the cloud provided darkness through which the Egyptians could not see to advance in the night. God can do anything, and He moved from being their guide leading the way, to being their rear-guard of protection. He moved the cloud from their front, and turned it into darkness behind them between the two camps for the protection of His people. They cried out to God and were spared from harm.

When God says go forward, He means not only has He made a chosen path for you, but that He will protect you from those things in the past trying to draw you back. Let go of the past! Move forward by faith trusting Him for the journey.

Is there something or somewhere you need to leave behind – something you need to forget! God says go forward. He will deliver you from the pain of the past if you will trust Him for the future. Pray Philippians 3:13-14 below to help you on your way.

Today's Prayer: *Heavenly Father, "...I press on, that I may lay hold of that for which Christ Jesus has also laid hold of me. I do not count myself to have apprehended it; but one thing I do, forgetting those things which are behind and reaching forward to those which are ahead, I press toward the goal for the prize of the upward call of God in Christ Jesus." Lord, help me to press on, Amen*

Tragedy to Triumph

"Josiah was eight years old when he became king, and he reigned in Jerusalem thirty-one years. He did what was right in the eyes of the LORD and walked in the ways of his father David, not turning aside to the right or to the left."
2 Chronicles 34:1-2

Scripture Reading: Second Chronicles 34

All too often responsibility falls upon the shoulders of those much too young to carry it. Such was the case with an eight year old boy whose name was Josiah. He became king at that young age due to tragedy – the assassination of his father. But this tragedy in his young life became a triumph for an entire nation of people.

When loss comes our way and responsibility is heaped upon us at a much too young age, there are choices to make. We can bend to the status quo and leave things as they are, or we can strive to be different seeking a better outcome than those before us. We can choose God and His ways in order to rise above the environment surrounding us.

That is what Josiah did. When he was sixteen, he began to seek the God of King David. Then when he was twenty, he began to tear down and get rid of the idols and pagan images in the land – those things that were not pleasing to God and were leading people astray. But it wasn't until he was twenty-six that the word of God was found in the temple, and that is when he read the covenant of the LORD to the people in the presence of God for the first time – *"...to follow the LORD and keep His commands, regulations and decrees with all his heart and all his soul, and to obey the words of the covenant written in His word."* His life and the lives of the nation of people were changed as they encountered the Lord and His word.

All of this occurred because a young man knew deep in his heart that the way they were living and the environment around him was not right. He wanted to be different. He wanted to rise above the circumstances. He didn't accept things as they were, but chose to make a difference seeking God's way instead of man's way. And so he purged the land of all that was not of God.

Wow! What an amazing story showing us that tragedy and age are not a barrier to being the person God wants you to be. The impact you can have on others is directly related to choices. You, too, can choose to seek the LORD in your time of tragedy. You can choose to rise above the circumstances. You can choose to use the circumstances in your life to make a difference in the lives of those around you as you choose to follow God's way rather than the way things have been or may be. Choose Christ, He is the only way to the Father, and He is the way to the healing of a broken heart.

"Jesus said to him, *'I am the way, the truth, and the life. No one comes to the Father except through Me.'"* John 14:6

Today's Prayer: *Lord, as I read about a teenage boy who sought you even when he had never seen your word, I am humbled. And so I am seeking you right now and choosing to read your word for direction in my life. I acknowledge my need for you and choose to be used by You to make a difference in this world in which I live. Help me to look beyond my own personal tragedy toward the future of rising above the circumstances. In Jesus name, I pray, Amen.*

When Fear Doesn't Win

*"The LORD therefore be judge and decide between
you and me; and may He see and plead my
cause, and deliver me from your hand."*
I Samuel 24:12

Scripture Reading: First Samuel 16:17-21

As I was reading the story of David in the Bible regarding a time when he was living in the king's palace, I couldn't help but think how his story relates to the lives of so many women we speak to in the ministry. The Bible says that King Saul brought David into his house to be his attendant and armor bearer. It says that Saul loved him greatly and that David found favor with the king.

However, later the king became jealous of David when the people began to speak highly of him, and the king tried to kill David – not just once, but several times. The first time King Saul threw his sword at David, David fled for his life. But as time went by, the king saw that the people loved David and so he lured him back into his home where he tried to kill him again. There is so much to be learned from David's response when jealousy caused betrayal and attempted murder on his life. First, he ran! Then, he didn't allow himself to be lured back again.

Living on the run, fearing for his life, was no easy task. But through it all his friend, Jonathan, defended him to his father, the king. He encouraged David in the Lord saying *"Do not be afraid because the hand of Saul my father shall not find you, and you will be king over Israel and I will be next to you…"* First Samuel 23:16-17

There may be moments in your life when betrayal has caused you to be afraid, or when someone else's jealous rage has caused you to run from the situation. Perhaps it is someone you have loved and supported, who said they loved you, but became violent because of jealousy. What can you learn from David's story to help you get past the pain, fear and disruption to your life?

- **Be practical!** David's response to the threats on his life was practical. He left the scene escaping the presence of the threat. First Samuel 18:11; 19:10 He was lured back once, but never again.

- **Be alert** and on guard. Jonathan told David his father was seeking to put him to death. He said, "*...please be on guard in the morning and stay in a secret place and hide yourself.*" First Samuel 19:3

- **Keep busy.** David's emotional response was fear, but his physical response was to continue in the task before him. In his case, he was a warrior and he continued to fight the battles in front of him. In today's terms, he went to work every day even while dealing with this crisis situation.

- **Listen to godly counsel.** David also responded spiritually. He sought the wisdom of a godly friend who encouraged him in the Lord. Jonathan was a friend to David who interceded on his behalf with the king, his father. He also counseled him with a plan for safety. First Samuel 20

- **Seek justice, not vengeance.** There was a time when David had opportunity to kill Saul. Instead of killing him, he did not seek his own vengeance but rather delivered him over to the Lord for justice. First Samuel 24:10-24

- **Pray.** *"Even though I walk through the valley of the shadow of death, I fear no evil; for Thou art with me..."* Psalm 23:4a

Today's Prayer. If you can relate to a situation like this, pray in this way. *Oh Lord, how I long to feel safe. Running from the circumstances of life has taken its toll on me. I pray that you will fill me with your wisdom in knowing what to do next. Help me to release any thoughts of revenge to you for your justice to be done. Lead me to godly counsel and help me to be practical and busy as I await justice to be served. Lord, I ask that you would replace my sense of fright with a since of safety and security. I thank you that my life is in your hands, and that your word promises to deliver me from evil for Thine is the kingdom, power and glory forever. Amen*

The Better Choice

"Our help is in the name of the LORD, the Maker of heaven and earth."
Psalm 124:8

Scripture Reading: Psalm 124

Throughout the Bible, we find stories where people suffered at the hands of others as a result of choices. Can you think of a time when this has occurred in your life?

In the age-old story of Adam and Eve in Genesis One, we find the first people who suffered as a result of a decision to listen to an ungodly influence rather than remember and act upon the word of God. They suffered the spiritual pain of guilt and separation from God as well as physical pain of childbirth for Eve and lifelong hard labor for Adam. But in addition, they suffered the emotional pain of having a son murdered by his own brother.

The choice they made early in life set the tone for the rest of their lives and all the generations to follow. With their decision to act upon an ungodly influence, evil gained a foothold in the world through sin.

I remember a time in my teenage years when I was influenced by ungodly advice and made a decision that cost me dearly setting me on a path of ungodly choices for a long time. The pain of looking back and wishing things were different caused suffering for many years.

Then I met someone who told me about choosing a relationship that was forgiving, loving and forever. That relationship is with God through the Lord Jesus Christ. He is the only One who can make all things new to enable us to forget those things behind and press on toward His call on our lives. He washes us clean and not only forgives the past, but forgets it as well.

In a relationship with Christ, the only way the past can destroy your life and relationships is by listening to the same voice that influenced Eve in the Garden of Eden. That voice is from Satan himself. He is the one who tries to steal, kill and destroy your life of peace and joy in Christ and with others. But Jesus purifies our hearts to live in freedom from the bondage to past ungodly choices. He is the way out of the pull to drag us down and remind us constantly of all we have suffered. A relationship with Him gives us the ability to experience joy and peace even when the world's relationships are trying to rip us apart.

I love the words of Psalm 124:2-3 which say *"If the LORD had not been on our side when men attacked us, then they would have swallowed us alive in their burning anger against us."* And in verse eight above, we find the promise from God; *"our help is in the name of the LORD, the Maker of heaven and earth."*

God is our help in those times we suffer as a result of our past choices. And we suffer because we cannot go back and change the past. We cannot go back in time and make a different decision. But we can make the better choice today – and that is to choose Jesus.

Life is all about choices. What we choose today will impact the future for us and those we love. We can choose to be bitter or better. We can choose to be forgiving or forever holding a hurt. We can choose to love or to hate. We can choose to listen to ungodly advice or the still, small voice of God. What is the better choice? God forgives, loves and provides a better way of living as we listen to His Word. Choose to love, forgive and listen to the will of God. Choose Jesus for the healing of your soul.

Today's Prayer: *Father, forgive me for the wrong choices I have made in my past. Help me to make choices for the future that honor you and serve your purpose in my life. Amen*

Compassion Motivates Action

"But a certain Samaritan who was on a journey, came
upon him; And when he saw him, he felt compassion..."
Luke 10: 33

Scripture Reading: Luke 10:29-37

In identifying the theme of Luke 10:30-37, you discover that compassion is a major portion of this passage. As you read all of the verses, you see that it was out of compassion that the physical action took place which gave emotional support enabling a spiritual result.

In looking at the word compassion as used in scripture, it actually means "a tender and sensitive love, sympathy, pity, mercy". It is something that God grants and makes us the objects of according to Genesis 43:14 and Psalm 106:46. Compassion is felt when a need is revealed. The need is often accompanied by pain and/or grief, and compassion is a way for God's tender mercies to be extended through His people.

When a person is hurting, there is nothing wrong with asking God to extend compassion. When you pray for His mercies and praise Him that they are new every morning, you are actually asking for His compassion to be given to you. God's tender mercies come your way through the lives of those you meet in your times of need.

From the Old Testament to the New Testament, you will find the compassion of God to His people even when they had turned away from Him. He is a loving and compassionate God; therefore, He shows compassion. Deuteronomy 4:29-31. It is out of His compassion that He is gracious and slow to anger. The Bible tells us that He extends His compassion to:

- the poor and needy - Isaiah 58:7

- the rebellious and fearful - Nehemiah 9:17-19

- the distressed and depressed – Matthew 9:36

- those who suffer – James 5:11

- those who mourn – Isaiah 61:2

- those who are sick - Matthew 10:1

God is love and as such always puts compassion first. Lamentations 3:22 tells us that His compassions never fail and are new every morning. Great is His faithfulness. We are blessed to be able to experience the compassion of God in our lives personally as we experience our own times of pain, sorrow, depression and distress and even our sinfulness.

But there is a journey of compassion that we exhibit toward others who are hurting as we follow the example of the Good Samaritan. Not only are you able to exhibit compassion by God's grace, but you are told to do it. In reading Psalm 103:4, you find that God crowns you with love and compassion. You have it on your head! He has covered your mind and thoughts with His compassion; therefore, you are able to know how to extend it toward others. He has given it to you, not only for your benefit in times of suffering, but for the benefit of others through you. Because of God's love for you, a crown rests upon your head – a crown of compassion.

When you come upon a person in need, someone who is hurting, and you feel compassion, allow it to motivate you to action. Respond to the needs of others and you will be blessed.

Today's Prayer: *Lord, thank you for your mercies toward the hurting. Help me to be more compassionate toward others. Amen.*

Going Fishing

"...throw your net on the right side of the boat and you will find some."
John 21:6a

Scripture Reading: John 21:6-13

On a vacation with our adult children, grandsons and other family members, the boys kept disappearing for long periods of time. They had found a place to fish and spent most of the trip catching fish. They were amazed that almost every time they threw their line in, they caught big fish. They had a great time and took lots of photos to show their friends at home.

In John 21, some of the disciples of Jesus were fishing and not catching anything. You may read it and think "so they didn't catch any fish – it's nice they had time to fish". But we need to understand this was not a vacation day for them. It was a work day. Catching fish was their work – their livelihood. For them, not catching fish would be the same as our working hard and not receiving a paycheck. And so you can imagine their frustration and grumbling empty stomachs.

Then something amazing happened. Jesus stood on the shore and called out to them, *"friends haven't you any fish"*. When they said no, He told them to throw their net on the other side of the boat – the right side. When they did, their catch was so huge the net was full. And then Jesus told them to bring it to him where He had a fire and they would have breakfast. He then fed them bread and fish. Jesus met their need and more!

How do you feel when you have been doing your job, working as hard as you know how; and yet, seeing no results? If you are like most people, you probably feel frustrated, discouraged and even fearful if your livelihood depends on what you are doing.

There are several important things to note from the passage that can help us in our times of frustration and fear about future provisions.

- They had an unmet need – v5

- Jesus saw their need and gave them instruction – v6

- They listened – v6

- They did what He said – v6

- They listened again – v10

- They gave according to what He asked – v11

- Jesus gave to meet their need – v12-13

Working on relationships can be just as frustrating as fishing without a catch. When working on it and thinking you are doing what you are supposed to, yet see no change in response, something must not be right. Perhaps there is a way of reconciliation we haven't tried and that is Jesus' way – the right way.

Jesus gave instruction to the disciples and they listened! So often we are so busy doing what is in front of us that we miss the word from our Lord when all He wants is to give us instruction for filling our nets and getting life right to satisfy our needs. He says, *"...throw it to the right side".* Apparently, they spent a lot of time working on the wrong side of the boat! Throwing is doing according to the instruction of Christ. And so what is it that is causing you misery and frustration? What are you spending a lot of time doing that is opposite from God's right? Is it an unforgiving heart? Then, do the opposite; forgive. Is it unresolved anger? Do the opposite; ask forgiveness. Is it trying to carry all your problems alone instead of listening to Jesus? Do the opposite; pray and study God's word. Is it solving life's problems on your own; ask Him for help.

If our lives are not getting the results we hoped for or expected, listening and doing according to God's word is the answer for having needs met. Our plan of action should be to go fishing with Jesus. Listen, do, give and we have a promise from His word that He will meet every need. Ask Him in your prayer today.

I was so proud of our grandsons with their catch. They didn't need the fish and so they gave them back so others with a need could benefit from the catch. That is what Jesus asks of us – to give back. He then honors our giving by meeting our every need.

Today's Prayer: *Jesus, I thank you for your presence in my life and ask you to speak to my heart with instruction for my work and relationships. Show me the way to having needs met that are causing me frustration, exhaustion and insecurity and give me the strength and courage to do as you instruct. Help me to trust you enough to give it all to you. Thank you for meeting my needs every day. Amen*

Fighting Tomorrows Battle

"...Thus says the LORD to you: Do not be afraid
nor dismayed because of this great multitude,
for the battle is not yours, but Gods."
Second Chronicles 20:15

Scripture Reading: Second Chronicles 20:1-24

We have all had occasions in our lives when we knew a battle was brewing; perhaps in the home, in the office, even at church or in our own minds and emotions. And when a battle is brewing, knowing that we have to face it head on tomorrow is enough to send us running backward in time hoping tomorrow won't come too quickly.

In our ministry to people who have suffered loss, we have seen time and again how difficult it is for them to move forward because they are still walking backward looking at the loss behind them. In order for healing to begin, it is important to reach that place of turning around toward the future. But facing the future is a battle of fear and emotion.

And there is much we can learn from King Jehoshaphat through the above passage as the enemy gathered in a great multitude against his kingdom. Instead of rushing out to fight the battle unprepared, he took several steps of preparation first. The Kingdom of Judah had suffered great loss in the past, but this King knew what to do in order to face the coming battle.

First, according to verse 2, even though he was afraid the first thing he did was to seek the Lord in prayer and instruct the entire kingdom to do the same. His prayer is found in verses 5-12. He recounted to the Lord all He had done for them. He stated what the Kingdom of Judah had done in obedience to the Lord. Then he presented the problem... *"And now here are these people coming to throw us out of Your possession which you have given us, and God we have no power over them. Won't you judge them?"* Feelings of powerlessness are common in those who suffered in the past.

And then in verse 15 is a word of promise from the Lord to the Kingdom of Judah that we can still claim in the battles we face personally. The Lord said, *"Do not be afraid nor dismayed because of this great multitude, for the battle is not yours, but God's."* What this says to people now is, the battle you face tomorrow is not yours! You can claim this promise as you face the future.

The Lord continued with instruction, *"Tomorrow go down against them... you will not need to fight in this battle. Position yourselves, stand still and see the salvation of the LORD who is with you."* In other words, turnaround from the past and face the future; for I, the Lord, am promising you that this battle is mine. I will fight it for you!"

But after the word of the Lord and before the Kingdom of Judah faced tomorrow, they worshiped the Lord, and they sang praises to Him. What was the result? I love this part!! When the people began to sing and praise God, the Lord set ambushes against their enemy. Do you see what has happened? While the Kingdom of Judah praised God, He was fighting their battle for them! So when tomorrow came, there was no fight there!

What an encouragement is found in this example. When looking behind you is causing you fear, God says, turn around and face tomorrow. You have a promise from His word that He will fight for you. But the first thing you must do in order to move forward with hope and healing is to pray, acknowledge the problem, and ask God to work in it. Then worship His Holy Name and sing praises to Him. As you praise Him, you can know that He is in the midst of your battle making a way for your tomorrow whether it be a battle of emotions or relationships or something else. Oh, how I praise His name!

Today's Prayer: *Father, you are greatly to be praised for you are holy, just and righteous in all your ways. Glory and honor I do give to Thee. Thank you for going before us and preparing the way to freedom. With You fighting our battles for us, there is nothing to fear. Praise You. Amen*

When Wounds Cut Deep

"He heals the brokenhearted and binds up their wounds."
Psalm 147:3

Open wounds attract germs and dirt that cause an infection. When this happens, it can seem that healing takes forever. If the wound is not cleaned and bandaged properly, there is danger of the infection spreading to other parts of the body. The entire body suffers because of an untreated wound. An infected wound festers and appears red and angry because it is trying on its own to fight off the infection.

Internal wounds of the heart work much the same way. When wounds of the heart have been cut too deep for immediate healing, those wounds not only affect our entire body and mind, but the lives of those around us. They are wounds that have been cut deep from verbal and physical abuse, rejection, sorrow, loss or anything that assaults the emotions. These wounds can actually cause the heart to physically hurt. Anyone who has experienced this kind of pain knows exactly what I am talking about. A wound that cuts this deep requires something more than a Band-Aid and a good night's sleep. This pain is not one that will heal itself.

And so, how do you treat a broken and wounded heart? The most important thing you can do is to know deep within your heart that God knows your pain and is near to you as you go through it. We have His promise in Psalm 34:18. *"The LORD is near to the brokenhearted, and saves those who are crushed in spirit."* In this verse, the word brokenhearted actually means broken into pieces, to crush, destroy, quench, tear and burst.

I'm sure we have all had those occasions in life when we have been hurt, but the word brokenhearted implies a heart that has been shattered into pieces. And for something broken that severely, it will take spiritual and professional help to put all the pieces together again.

I remember years ago when my husband was trimming the hedges with a power trimmer. He accidently hit his finger cutting it to the bone. We bandaged the cut and went about our business. We were young and didn't realize the extent of the wound. Very soon it became apparent that our bandage was not going to be enough. The wound would not stop bleeding. He needed the help of emergency professionals to stitch up the cut properly so it could begin to heal.

Because we cannot see the wounds of the heart, we don't think of it in the same way. And yet, a severely wounded heart requires help to stitch up the cut so it will begin to heal. And so to experience healing of the heart, first accept that God is near. He is your emergency room physician, and the only one who can stitch up your shattered heart.

However, seek godly professional help if you are unable to focus on healing from the Lord. Then claim God's promise of healing. God is not only near to the brokenhearted, but Psalm 147:3 tells us that *"He heals the brokenhearted."* God has the power and ability to save us from anything which brings us harm. We may suffer for a season, but the Lord redeems the soul of those who take refuge in Him.

Today's Prayer: *Father, my heart is shattered and broken and needs to be stitched back together again. Today I am placing my pain in Your hands and claiming your promise of healing. Thank you for being near to me in my pain. It brings me great comfort to know that you are near and that you care what happens to me. Amen*

Calm the Raging Sea

"Then they called on the LORD and said, "We earnestly pray, O LORD, do not let us perish on account of this man's life and do not put innocent blood on us; for Thou, O LORD hast done as Thou hast pleased."
Jonah 1:14

Scripture Reading: Jonah 1:1-2:1

God gave Jonah an assignment which he not only ran from, but refused to be a participant. His answer to God's assignment was to run and to shut out the world around him. Innocent people suffered as a result of his attitude and actions while he escaped physically on a ship and emotionally in sleep. Someone had to wake him up and tell him of the disaster happening around him before he realized the damage he was causing to others.

Even Jonah's response was self-directed; "just throw me overboard." He acknowledged to them that the disaster was his fault, but he did not acknowledge to God sorrow for his actions that brought about the suffering of others. He did not pray for the others and for their deliverance. What he did was to direct the focus to himself rather than to God. "If I martyr myself, the sea will become calm – oh woe is me."

What is interesting in this story is the response of those men on the ship. When Jonah told them to throw him overboard, they just couldn't bring themselves to do it. They were very afraid, but they tried to row for shore rather than sacrifice his life. When that didn't work, they (not Jonah) called on the Lord and prayed they would not perish on account of Jonah's life. They asked God not to put his blood on their hands. It was only after they prayed that they threw Jonah into the sea.

Immediately the sea stopped raging. The men were in awe of the Lord and offered sacrifice and made vows to the Lord. It was then that God sent a giant fish to save Jonah.

God's response to the actions and prayers of the men on board the ship was to immediately calm the sea, and to save Jonah. He answered the prayers of these frightened men. The amazing thing is that there is no record of Jonah praying until he had been in the stomach of the fish for three days. He spent a lot of time running from God and causing disaster in the lives of others before he finally decided to pray.

There are lessons to learn in this story from two points of view. The first is that you cannot run from God. When He has an assignment for you, whether you agree with the task or not, you cannot run from it. Point number two is that even though you may have been suffering as a result of the actions of others, even though their actions have created fear and pain, you can still pray for that person and for the circumstances. You can still do what must be done in order to save your life and those around you who are in your care. Prayer is a powerful tool for courage, wisdom and salvation. Prayer calms the raging sea like nothing else can, especially a prayer for someone who has caused you distress.

Today's Prayer: *"Father, I thank you for showing me how important it is to pray for those who have caused disaster in my life and in the*

lives of those around me. Today I pray for _____ that you will not hold their actions against me, and that you will save them from the consequences of their actions. Turn their life around for your glory. Amen.

A Fear That Calms

*"I would have despaired unless I had believed that
I would see the goodness of the LORD in the land of
the living. Wait for the LORD. Be strong, and let your
heart take courage; yes, wait for the LORD."*
Psalm 27:13-14

Scripture Reading: Psalm 27, John 3:16

When everything within you screams that life is unfair, I pray that you have somehow been able to see the goodness of God even in your despair as you have read and prayed through this section on overcoming fear. If you are reading this, you are alive, and that means you can experience God's goodness because you are in the land of the living. Fear not – God is with you.

And as we conclude this first section of devotionals for your hurting heart on the topic of fear, there is one type of fear we have not talked about. In Psalm 31:19, we read *"how great is the goodness of God for those who fear Him."* You mean we are to be afraid of God? That is not what it says. It says to fear Him. This kind of fear is not that of terror, but that of reverence – to be in reverent awe of a Holy God.

This kind of fear is based on belief. It is based on faith in God through His Son, Jesus Christ. It is this kind of faith that gives courage and strength to face the negative fears in life. It is this kind of fear that gives hope in the place of despair.

Do you believe in God? Notice in today's key verse above that it was belief in the Lord that conquered despair in the life of the Psalmist so that he was strong and courageous. Do you believe God loves you? Do you believe in His goodness and salvation? Do you believe in the Lord Jesus Christ?

John 3:16 says this, *"For God so loved the world, that He gave His only begotten Son, that whoever believes in Him should not perish, but have everlasting life."*

If you have not yet placed your faith and trust in Jesus as Savior to believe in Him and secure your place in Heaven, I want to encourage you to do so now. The following prayer will guide you... pray it now.

Today's Prayer: *Lord Jesus, I want to place my trust in you. I confess that my life has not been all it should be, and that I have sinned in my life according to your word. Please forgive me and come into my life today as my Lord and Savior. I believe that you are God's Son and I long to see your goodness replace the despair that has come as a result of grief and fear. Thank you for loving me. Amen*

Section Two

Quenching the Flames of Anger

Who by faith… "…*quenched the power of fire*".
Hebrews 11:34a

Beginning the Journey to Restoration Out of Anger

"You have tried my heart, you have visited me by night, you have tested me and have found nothing; I have purposed that my mouth will not transgress."
Psalm 17:3

Writing these devotionals on the topic of anger has been one of the most difficult assignments the Lord has given me. It has been a struggle to look at the causes, reactions and results of the devastation left in the wake of anger. It has gripped me with unreasonable outbursts that I haven't understood. It has taken me longer to complete the project than any assignment before this. And I have to be honest and say that, "I can't wait to be finished with it"! But even with the difficulty, I have known that God was at work and would complete the project in His own time – not without teaching me a few things first! And He can do the same with you. The end result of freedom is worth the effort of working day by day toward that goal.

We had just returned from a week's vacation – the first we had taken in many years. It was to be a time of relaxation and inspiration. When I travel, I always look forward to the inspiration God gives for writing and spending time with Him. Each day of our trip I waited, expecting that great 'ah ha' moment. It didn't come. In fact, it seemed that there was a block in my mind preventing me from being able to think a rational thought. I couldn't understand it. I wanted to hear from God, I was in a beautiful place for being inspired, but it just didn't happen. In addition, I was having trouble sleeping that week and the weeks following our return.

As I returned home, I asked the Lord to reveal to me what was blocking me from hearing His voice. Several days later it became clear. It was anger. I recognized it, I struggled with it, and just when I felt like expressing it, I sensed the still small voice of God saying, "Be silent – just wait." Each day that week as I drove to and from work, my thoughts were totally negative and grumbling. Amazingly, I kept my mouth shut and my thoughts to myself!

On one of those mornings, I read from *Experiencing God Day-By-Day* by Henry and Richard Blackaby. From their devotional titled *Making Necessary Adjustments*, one statement stood out to me. It says, "Satan will try to convince you that obedience carries much too high a price, but he will never tell you the cost of not obeying God. If you are to be used in God's service you must expect to make adjustments in your life." Adjustments and obedience - two words that pack a wallop! It was no accident that I read these words at that time. I knew that if I was to move forward, I had to adjust and obey God's plan for me.

After several days of struggle, I asked a friend to pray for me because I was struggling with an issue. That afternoon, as I was driving home, my thoughts began to lay out the plan of salvation in my mind. I thought about our adoption into God's family through the blood of the Lamb, Jesus Christ. I thought of redemption, how we were bought with a price, Christ's blood which was shed for us once for all, and how we are forgiven because of the riches of His grace.

This is what is interesting. That morning I was looking for anything that would help me to focus on something besides negative issues.

I opened a set of CD's that are the reading of the New Testament. I listened to one before I arrived at the office and requested prayer from my friend. So, the same CD was still playing as I was driving home. As I was thinking about what Christ has done for us, suddenly, the very thoughts I was thinking were being read from the CD. The exact words! I was stunned. My thought came before the reading, how cool is that! When I got home, I opened my Bible to Ephesians Chapter One to read what I heard on the CD. Sure enough, in my drive time, I was quoting verses from Ephesians without even realizing it. I couldn't wait to share with my friend what God had done and to thank her for her prayers.

Often what we don't realize as we struggle with something is that God is at work in our hearts and minds even though we don't feel that He is. He knows the issues we deal with. He knows any loss we have experienced. What I had forgotten is that I had prayed several weeks before telling God that I felt inadequate to complete the devotional section on anger when I still had issues with it myself. I told God I felt like a phony. So, He took me through a process and experience of resolution in order to help walk me and others through the process of surviving and overcoming the negative impact of anger. The following is the path I experienced in order to overcome.

- Situation occurred leading to anger

- Negative thoughts blocked inspiration

- Struggle followed

- God shut my mouth

- Adjustment, obedience

- Sought positive input

- Sought prayers of friend

- God filled my mind with His Word

- God made His presence known through His Word

- Prayers answered

- Issue resolved

It seems simple when you can put it into a list, but have no doubt, dealing with negative emotions in your heart and mind is a process – and a difficult one at that. It takes time.

Today's Prayer: *Thank you Lord for hearing and answering my prayers. In those times of struggle when we know the right thing to do but delay in obedience, you patiently take us through the process toward obedience. Dealing with unresolved anger is not easy, but you Lord are faithful to stay the course through it as I struggle. Thank you for taking away the negative and replacing it with your powerful and positive words of promise. Amen.*

Turning Your Mad to Glad

*"It was for freedom that Christ set us free; therefore keep
standing firm and do not be subject again to a yoke of slavery."*
Galatians 5:1

Scripture Reading: Galatians 5

We have probably all heard at one time or another, the phrase,
"Don't be mad, be glad." Just hearing the phrase makes me mad!
But here is the thing. You cannot be glad about anything until
you deal with the issues you are mad about. And being glad about
anything requires a level of peace, which has been interrupted by
being mad. How can you get that peace?

And so, for the remainder of the book, you will be reading about
people in the Bible who were angry, as well as people around us
today who are angry. You will read about God dealing with anger
in others, and His own anger. And you will learn where the peace
comes from that will overcome the anger.

As I have put together these readings, I have jokingly told others
I will be glad to finish, because I am tired of having to deal with
being mad! But the reality is none of us can move past anger
without dealing with the issues of it, in order to move through the
anger. My prayer for you is that God will do a mighty work in your
heart, and that you will allow him to reveal those hidden places of
the heart that are hindering you from a life of hope and peace.

Today, as you begin, ask God to help you identify, address, and
move beyond being angry all the time and to fill your heart

with the peace that only He can give. It is the only way to move beyond a life controlled by anger to live in the hope and joy that He wants you to have. And believe me when I say, I know this to be true.

One of the most convicting verses in the Bible for me has been from Galatians 5:7-8, "*You were running well; who hindered you from obeying the truth? This persuasion did not come from Him who calls you.*" I have learned in my life that anger hinders. It is as simple as that. It stops me from being able to see what God wants in my life. It is not fueled by God, but rather by the enemy of God who wants to defeat us from living lives of peace and joy. Why? Peace and joy nurture and build relationships, but anger destroys them. The goal of the devil is to destroy our lives and relationships, hindering us from being effective in the work of Christ.

And so as you read through the devotionals in this section, keep asking yourself these things:

- Why am I mad?

- What is my being angry accomplishing for good?

- Is my anger destroying personal relationships?

- Do I want to be different and how can I change?

May God's wisdom and mercy guide you to a greater understanding of who you are in Him, and how to replace any angry thoughts and actions in your life with a loving and forgiving spirit of peace.

Today's Prayer: *Lord, help me to be able to address any thoughts and emotions that are controlling my life in a negative way. If it is anger, please reveal that to me and show me how to identify the reason and the solution for it. Thank you, Lord Jesus. Amen.*

Angry at God

"But it greatly displeased Jonah and he became angry."
Jonah 4:7

Jonah was a prophet God used to send a wakeup call to people who were living a violent and evil lifestyle. When the people heard the message of coming judgment from Jonah, they turned from their evil and violent ways and turned to God. The Bible calls this repentance. When people are truly repentant, sorry for their actions, turning away from them and turning to God, He extends mercy. That is what happened with the people of Nineveh. God did not destroy the city and the people living there because they repented and turned to Him.

However, since Jonah had delivered a message of destruction as God had instructed, he became angry at God when He showed mercy instead of the judgment Jonah had preached. Rather than rejoicing in all the lives that were saved as a result of repentance, Jonah became angry because the judgment and punishment for the evil actions of man he expected was not given.

Can you relate to Jonah's attitude? When those who have wronged us, or wronged those we love, do not get what they deserve, we tend to be much more judgmental than God, and therefore, angry at the injustice we see around us. Jonah was so mad that he lashed out at God and wanted to die. He was angry at the grace, compassion, and mercy shown to unrighteous people.

76

Has there been a time when you felt this way? Have you felt angry at God for showing mercy to those who do not deserve it? Have you felt judgmental – lashing out and wanting to die because life is not fair?

Jonah's attitude needed an overhaul, and there are seasons in life when ours may need an adjustment as well. Look again at Jonah 4:2 and the descriptive words Jonah used to describe God. He said, "I know that you are…"

- Gracious

- Compassionate

- Slow to anger

- Abounding in mercy

- One who relents concerning judgment

Rather than being angry, Jonah would have been better off to focus on these attributes of God and to thank Him for them. If God shows these attributes to those who have been violent and evil, how much more will He give to those who have been wounded by that type of person? Take a moment to thank God for His grace, compassion, and mercy toward you today. Even in your anger, God is slow to be angry with you. Pray as the Psalmist did…

Today's Prayer: *"O God, arrogant men have risen up against me, and a band of violent men have sought my life, and they have not set You before them. But You, O LORD, are a God merciful and gracious, slow to anger and abundant in loving kindness and truth.*

Turn to me, and be gracious to me; Oh grant Your strength to Your servant and save the son of Your handmaid. Show me a sign for good, that those who hate me may see it and be ashamed, because You, LORD, have helped me and comforted me." Psalm 86:14-17

Abundant in Mercy

"For You, LORD, are good and ready to forgive, and
abundant in mercy to all who call upon You."
Psalm 86:5

Scripture Reading: Psalm 86

In thinking back to Jonah's story from the previous devotional, you find that God did not destroy a city of sinful people because they repented and turned back to Him. This reflects God's character of patience and mercy. He is slow to anger. When we turn against Him through our actions or attitudes, He gives us every opportunity to change the direction of our lives by seeking Him again. If you are inclined to think that God is angry with you, think again. He is not only slow to anger, but abundant in love, kindness and mercy. That means He gives to you a whole, great big bunch of love and mercy which covers a multitude of sin.

Circumstances over which we have no control can cause us to become angry. And out of that anger, actions that are not very attractive for a Christian will occur. I remember doing something out of anger that I was later so ashamed of doing that I cried my regret and sorrow to the Lord and the other person. I knew I had acted inappropriately and damaged my witness for Christ. But as I sat humbly before the Lord, I knew the sorrow over my sin was what God expected and wanted of me, but not once did I sense that God was angry with me. Disappointed – yes, but not angry. I know He loves me and is patient with me. Does that excuse my actions and words – no, it does not. There was a requirement of me as a result of my actions, and that was to seek God's forgiveness and to seek the forgiveness of the other person.

In Psalm 86:5, it says that God is full of mercy toward those who call upon Him. Just as He showed mercy toward Nineveh, He showed mercy to me. And God's mercy toward you is abundant as well – a whole, great big bunch poured out especially for you.

In times of anger, focusing on the mercy, love, and kindness of the Lord is what will take you beyond anger to a place of peace. His promise is one of compassion for you

Today's Prayer: *Lord, the standard of Your character is where I need to direct my focus. Help me to do so in a way that controls my negative emotions toward You and toward others. Amen*

Putting Things in Perspective

"...should I not have compassion on Nineveh?"
Jonah 4:77

"Do you have good reason to be angry?" Jonah was so angry that he wanted to die. But what God recognized in him was an outburst of anger for a surface issue that covered a deeper problem. The surface issue was a plant that had died. The real issue was Jonah's attitude toward God over circumstances that he could not control. He was still angry that God showed mercy instead of judgment for Nineveh, but the anger he expressed was related to taking away his comfort. His attitude was so resentful and despondent that he no longer wanted to live.

There was a pattern of behavior in the life of Jonah that God was trying to get him to acknowledge and change. His attitude led him to a place of despair and self-pity. Jonah was trying to control God and His actions, so the results would be the way he thought they should be, rather than according to God's character of mercy and compassion. God's point to Jonah was the value of life. He pointed out that Jonah was angry over the death of one insignificant plant, but God was concerned with the lives of 120,000 people.

This story is a picture of how anger distorts our thinking until we have unrealistic expectations of others and of God. When those expectations are not met, emotions plunge to despair. As difficult as it may be for us, God wants us to put things in perspective. Whatever it is that has caused our anger, we may never know the why or the circumstance which caused it. And so, in order to survive this frame of mind, there are several things to do that help in getting our emotions to a place of healing.

- Acknowledge that God is wiser and more powerful that you are – Isaiah 40:21-27

- Identify the root of the anger before you become bitter - Hebrews 12:15

- Give your emotions and circumstances to God – Psalm 55:22, Psalm 69:19

- Be forgiving and merciful – Ephesians 4:32

- Re-join the land of the living – Matthew 22:32, 37

Today's Prayer: *Lord, Your wisdom and power are greater than anything my mind can comprehend. Please forgive my anger and take control of my emotions that I may be forgiving and merciful as You have been to me. Amen.*

Does God Get Mad

"God is a just judge, and God is angry with the wicked every day."
Psalm 7:11

Perhaps you or someone you know has been impacted by the violent behavior of a stranger or someone close to them. More than likely, you have witnessed the anger of those who were on the receiving end of the violent behavior. Anger is a normal reaction to a loss – loss of life, loss of home, loss of innocence, loss of dignity. But, there is hope and help for overcoming an anger that completely controls your life. You are not the only one angry at the crime done against you. God is angry with the wicked every day. He gets angry on your behalf.

Your anger is appropriate when it is directed toward the violent perpetrator against you. However, what you find in Psalm 7 is that God is for the righteous people who are being impacted by the evil intent of others. He is the Judge! *"The Lord shall judge the people"* (Psalm 7:8). He is your defense. He is the jury preparing for the punishment of the perpetrator. Knowing this relieves you of the need to hold onto your anger indefinitely.

The caution found here is to be careful that anger does not fester into a condition that interrupts your state of righteousness. Do not allow the wicked to take away your integrity through angry thoughts of revenge against them. If you are a victim of the evil intent and actions of others, verses 14-16 give insight into what the end result will be for perpetrators of violence. Even if they

83

have never been caught for the crime against you, never doubt that they will pay for their actions. God will not allow evil to go unpunished.

In Psalm 7, the psalmist is addressing his situation by calling on God as Judge to act on his behalf. He knows that God is on his side and will seek justice; therefore, he does not have to seek justice. The state of his trust in God and of his mind is reflected in verse 17 as he sings praise to God. This one simple verse indicates that he was at peace in knowing God would take care of the situation. It is similar to a young child being bullied or hurt and you, as a parent, coming to their defense making certain the parents of the bully know exactly what happened. Your child's heart is no longer troubled knowing that you were angry on their behalf and did something about it. God is your Heavenly Father. He is your parent. He cares about what has happened to you. And so you, too, can experience peace as you know and understand that God is for you in the midst of your situation. He is angry on your behalf, therefore, you do not have to be. Pray as the Psalmist did…

Today's Prayer: *Lord, I praise You according to Your righteousness and will sing praise to the name of the LORD Most High. Today, I am acknowledging You as Judge, and thank You for intervening on my behalf to see that the actions against me are vindicated. Cleanse my heart of anger so that I do not become as those who are against You. Be my defense and fill my heart with Your peace. In Jesus name, I pray, Amen.*

Unmet Expectations

"But now my eye sees You; therefore I retract,
and I repent in dust and ashes."
Job 42:5b-6

Scripture Reading: Job 1, 42

Remember as children, there were certain needs provided in our lives. But, in addition to needs, all children have dreams of what they want to be when they grow up, or how life will be different when they grow up. Children look forward to their dreams being fulfilled as they become adults.

However, life is not that predictable. Often you find adults who have been disappointed with unmet expectations in their lives and are still trying to live as children chasing dreams. The frustration of unfilled dreams causes an anger deep inside that was not caused by others, but is unleashed upon others. This anger is planted so deep and has been part of a life for so long, that you do not even realize it is there. It is so much a part of you that it is like you were born with it! You forget what life was like before you felt that way. Getting beyond this kind of anger requires facing reality. The "what should have been, or could have been if only..." must be dealt with because that thought process is not emotionally healing.

In the book of Job, you find a man whose expectations were not met due to losses in his life which would devastate anyone. He was married with sons and daughters. He was prosperous. He knew God and thought of himself as a righteous man. His expectation was to live that way forever. But something so horrendous happened to him that to even imagine it would bring a man down. His children were all killed. His livelihood was destroyed, and his health declined into extreme pain all the time. Adding insult to injury, Job's friends judged him to be in this state because of his own sin. It was at that point that Job became angry. After all he had been through, I would have been angry too! To endure loss, and then to be falsely judged as being the cause of the situation is more than a person can bear, and anger occurs.

Job is described in God's Word as a "blameless and upright man" and yet, he had unmet expectations. You see, thinking nothing bad will happen to us because we are in a right relationship with God is not correct thinking. God never promised we would not have trouble, but He did promise that He would be with us in our troubles. (Psalm 46:1) But, if we convince ourselves we are immune to trouble, and then disaster strikes, we have set ourselves up for an anger that causes us to question our faith, and everything we think we know about God. It is in this situation that reality sets in, and we must face it. Reality number one – it happened. Reality number two – friends or family blame you. Reality number three – "I thought God would…, but He didn't." Reality number four – I'm mad!

The Bible tells us that Job was a righteous man. It was not his sin that caused his tragedy, but rather God's confidence in Job's ability to cope, survive and recover. But, the circumstances of loss and judging friends angered Job and changed his attitude.

So, how do you move forward from a reality check that reveals how you really think and feel? Job's recovery came as he had a face-to-face encounter with God that was different than any he had ever experienced before. God revealed Job's heart to him and addressed the real issues. He brought Job face-to-face with his attitude in order to bring about a heart change. It was only through looking within himself and changing his incorrect attitude that Job was able to recover. It was only when he acknowledged God as being in control that Job was able to recover. Also, it was only as Job prayed for those who had falsely judged him that he was able to recover. The result is found in Job 42:10, *"and the LORD restored the fortunes of Job when he prayed for his friends, and the LORD increased all that Job had two fold."*

It is difficult to come to the realization that something within us must change in order for restoration, especially when the loss was the life of loved ones or our own health. But God has confidence that you can cope, survive and recover the losses of life, or He would never have allowed it to happen. He knows your name! He knows your destiny. He knows the answers for you, so seek to know and understand that He alone is GOD. You can survive and overcome the despair of unmet expectations that caused anger as you acknowledge what has occurred, and what needs to occur in order to be restored once again.

And as you do, you have a promise from God's Word in James 1:12, *"Blessed is a man who perseveres under trial; for once he has been approved, he will receive the crown of life, which the Lord has promised to those who love Him."* Friend, the crown of life is yours for the taking as you live the tragedies of life with an attitude of love for God, allowing Him to give you the strength to endure without allowing anger to take root and permanently park in your heart. You can cope, survive and be restored. Praise to the Living Savior who makes it possible.

Today's Prayer: *Father, let me see deep within myself what expectations I have had that were not of Your plan for me. And then, Oh Lord, help me to confess the lofty thoughts I have had about myself and to acknowledge that I am not in control of my life, You are. May Your will be done precious Savior. Amen.*

Words of Acceptance

"Let the words of my mouth and the meditation of my heart be
acceptable in your sight, O Lord my Rock and my Redeemer."
Psalm 19:14

Scripture Reading: Numbers 12:1-8, 11

An angry person is a critical person of themselves and of others. A critical comment may stem from jealousy, which simmers until the anger behind it verbalizes with a critical comment about someone who is innocent of the thing of which they are being criticized. In Numbers 12:1-2, you find an example when the sister and brother of Moses criticized his wife. But the deeper problem, which came out of their mouths as criticism, was jealousy over the leadership of Moses. Envy and resentment fueled an angry and critical attitude. But, Aaron was convicted that this attitude was wrong and described it in verse 11 as sin and foolishness

If you are experiencing an attitude of criticism, examine your heart for the reason. Pray as the Psalmist did in Psalm 19:14. Memorize the verse in order to call upon this word to God at a moment's notice when confronted with the temptation to be critical. If you are asking God to let your words be acceptable to Him, and your attitude to be pleasing to Him, you will need to think before you speak. You will need to analyze your thoughts when resentments surface. Ask yourself, "Is God pleased with my attitude?" If your thoughts and words are an angry attempt to raise your status above God's chosen leadership as Miriam and Aaron were doing, God's answer is that it is sin and foolishness.

But, our God is a loving and forgiving God. He will forgive the criticism as you talk to Him and acknowledge the wrong of it as He did with Aaron. He will forgive as you ask Him to forgive you. By praying "let the words of my mouth be acceptable to you", He will fill your mouth with pleasing words. By praying "let the meditation of my heart be acceptable", He will help you to change the attitude of your heart. There is healing in pleasant words (Proverbs 16:24) and good medicine in a joyful heart (Proverbs 17:22).

Today's Prayer: *"Lord, I acknowledge the critical attitude of my heart and the unpleasant words that have left my mouth causing pain to others. I ask your forgiveness and theirs. Fill my mouth with words that will bring healing to the relationships I have damaged, and change my heart to be filled with contagious joy that will be medicine to the soul. You are my Rock, my Redeemer. I praise You."* In Jesus name, Amen.

When Anger Tries to Rule

*"Then Haman went out that day glad and pleased of
heart; but when Haman saw Mordecai in the king's gate,
and that he did not stand up or tremble before him,
Haman was filled with anger against Mordecai."*
Esther 5:9

Scripture Reading: Esther 5, Second Peter 1:4

In our nation, we have heard about, or perhaps experienced, cutbacks due to the state of the economy. Companies that we thought would be around forever have had to close their doors. An edict was given in advance for the demise of a company name, resulting in the death of jobs and traumatic loss of livelihood for thousands. Emotions run high in situations like this. How do you respond as a Christian when the death of something or someone you depend upon is announced in advance of the loss?

There is a story in the book of Esther about an edict that was given for the Jewish people. They were to be put to death and their name wiped away with them. This edict was given because of the hatred and anger of one man toward another. Haman, an evil official of the king's court, was filled with anger toward Mordecai, a Jew. Mordecai had a job at the king's gate and because He would not compromise his faith by bowing down to the evil authority, Haman tried, not only to get him fired, but to get rid of him altogether. What is it that directed Haman's anger toward God's man? His anger was directed by greed, pride and ego, which brought about evil intent to destroy another. When you read Esther 5:9-10, you find Haman's pride, anger, and dissatisfaction. His anger called for others to agree with his view and to plot with him a plan of action for the destruction of others.

As a believer, how can you respond to anger that results in a premeditated plan to destroy you? When you are going to work each day doing your job and someone tries to get rid of you in order to elevate themselves, what can you do?

When Mordecai heard of the original threat, he responded in three ways:

- Faith – He bowed only to God, prayed and fasted.

- Wise Action – He sent word to the Queen (his niece) for intervention with the king.

- Consistency – He did not waver in his faith, nor did he cower in fear. He showed up for work each day waiting for and trusting in God's intervention.

There is so much we can learn from the courage of Mordecai and Esther. Further, when you read Second Peter 1:4, you discover that through Christ you have escaped the corruption that is in this world by His divine power. That is a promise for every believer in Christ! And so when the premeditated plans of an angry and evil person come against you, God's Word says that you have already escaped the corruption in this world for a more excellent outcome by allowing the divine nature of Christ to rule in you. Does this mean others will not be against you because you are a Christian? No, it means you have the power within you to stand firm in your faith, take action toward a solution, and be consistent in showing courage rather than cowering in fear or reciprocating the anger.

God gives us the ability to face opposition with wisdom and courage, trusting Him for intervention.

Today's Prayer: *Lord, I know this world in which we live is filled with people intent on hurting others out of wounded pride. But I thank you that you have given us Your divine nature through Christ to respond with wisdom, faith, action and consistency in what we are called to do. Protect us as we are threatened with destruction out of someone's evil anger. Thank You Jesus. Amen.*

Pulling Down Strongholds

"For the weapons of our warfare are not carnal but mighty in
God for pulling down strongholds, casting down arguments and
every high thing that exalts itself against the knowledge of God,
bringing every thought into captivity to the obedience of Christ."
Second Corinthians 10:4-5

Scripture Reading: Second Corinthians 10:1-7,
Ephesians 6:13-18

Strongholds... what are they? In this same verse in the New
American Standard translation of the Bible, they are called
fortresses. Does that give you a better picture of something that
surrounds people and places for their protection? However, in a
like manner, a stronghold or fortress can also be used to imprison.
A stronghold can imprison the heart, preventing or blocking,
the healing that needs to take place in order to live a full and
productive life. Some fortresses are powerful because they cannot
be penetrated from the outside. When we try to reach a person
whose heart has been wounded and hardened by the stronghold
surrounding it, the love we try to share simply does not compute
to their heart and mind. In order to get to the heart with healing,
the fortress around it must be pulled down from within. It is
simply not something a person can do for someone else.

The key verses above give insight for how to begin the process
of breaking down the walls of the heart that are preventing you
from experiencing the love and joy that God has for you to enjoy.
My heart breaks when I realize how unfair it is that those who
have been victimized by the evil intent of man are the ones who

93

suffer, not only from the act of violence against them, but from the after effects of negative emotions. Of course, there will be anger. But over time, if the anger is not talked out and worked out – if it is internalized – it will become a fortress so strong around the heart that it destroys from the inside out. If we are to survive, we must pull down the strongholds, cast out arguments and bring our every thought captive to the obedience of Christ. You pull it down by identifying it for what it is. Address it by name and throw out any internal argument for why you should continue to allow it to control you, then pray asking God to help you to hold every thought captive to the obedience of Christ. Pull down the lies, replace them with truth.

We are told in Scripture about armor we are to put on as protection against those things that would otherwise destroy us. That protection is the armor of God! We are to take up this armor in order to withstand in the evil day (Eph 6:13-18). And need I mention that we are living in an evil day filled with violence never seen or heard of in the days of our youth.

If anger is surrounding your heart and mind as a stronghold, and you want to pull it down, you will need to immediately replace it with a protective stronghold. Surround your body with truth replacing every lie that has captured your mind. That truth is God's Word. Wear righteousness to cover your heart. Righteousness is a result of a relationship with Christ. Walk in the gospel of peace and hold the shield of faith in front of you to guard against recapture. Take seriously the helmet of salvation and the sword of the Spirit for these are the word of God. When these things become the strength of your life, you will be able to guard against strongholds of the heart that are destructive. For the believer in Christ, the Bible says we are mighty in God for pulling down strongholds.

Today's Prayer: *Lord, the anger controlling me is based on the lie that I could have…, should have and it wouldn't have happened… or that You or those around me don't care. I am confessing these as lies that are destroying me and asking for You to cleanse my heart and mind. I want to be free. I want to be healed. I want to consciously put on the armor of God as my stronghold of protection. Help me to do this, I pray, Amen.*

Section Two

Quenching Flames -
Breaking Down Anger

	Negative Impact	**Positive Impact**
A	Anguish of Loss and Grief	Acceptance and Adjustments in Life
N	Negative Input Impacts Future Response	New Way of Life
G	Grief's Response	Grace Abundant and Free
E	Enemy of the Soul	Encouragement for the Soul
R	Rejection Hurts	Redemptive Relationship

$\mathcal{A}$ = $\mathcal{A}$nguish of $\mathcal{L}$oss and $\mathcal{G}$rief

*"For it is not an enemy who reproaches me, then I could
bear it; nor is it one who hates me who has exalted himself
against me, then I could hide myself from him. But it is you,
a man my equal, my companion and my familiar friend."*
Psalm 55:12-13

Scripture Reading: Psalm 55

When betrayal causes the loss of a friend or loved one, the pain
and grief are so overpowering that you feel as if you will never
get beyond it. Then, you begin to resent the pain and the anguish
turns to anger.

The Psalmist said he could bear it if the anguish and terror of
death had fallen upon him by an enemy, but it did not. It was his
companion and familiar friend who had a grudge against him and
brought trouble to him.

But in his trouble, anguish and fear, the Psalmist did what needed
to be done to prevent anger from taking hold. He said, *"as for me,
I shall call upon God and the Lord will save me...He will hear my
voice...He will redeem my soul in peace from the battle which is
against me."* (Psalm 55:16-18)

If the anguish of rejection and betrayal has turned to anger in your
life, I want to encourage you to do as the Psalmist did – call upon
God. Cast your burden on Him. He will not only hear your pain,
He will fill your soul with peace. And that is what an angry heart
longs for – peace. Be at peace dear friend, call upon Him.

Today's Prayer: *God You are a God of peace. How it must grieve You to see your children at war with one another. Knowing that You experience grief when we turn against You helps me to trust You in taking care of me in my grief and loss. Help me to cope Lord; to know what to do to get past this loss in my life. I am casting my burden upon You Lord and pray for my heart to be filled with Your peace. Amen.*

N = Negative Input Impacts Future Response

*"And those passing by were hurling abuse at Him, wagging
their heads, and saying, "You who are going to destroy
the temple and rebuild it in three days, save Yourself!
You are the Son of God, come down from the cross."*
Matthew 27:39-40

Scripture Reading: Matthew 27

As Jesus hung on the cross for us, the people passing by abused
Him with words. They were not angry words. They were mocking
words. They were an attempt to prove to others that they were right,
and Jesus was wrong. They were in effect saying, "Who do you
think you are? You can't even do what you said you could do."

Words are so powerful. They have the ability to build up or tear
down. They can destroy or defend, encourage or defeat. The people
were trying to prove the defeat of Jesus.

We get angry at times for reasons we cannot identify. If you can't
determine the reason why you are angry, then it is probably buried
so deep from past years that it will take time and concentrated
effort to resolve. Abusive words and constant criticism received
can create an angry person and a negative attitude.

A negative attitude stifles peace and joy by blocking you from
being able to heal from past abusive words. Is there hope for
victims of physical and emotional abuse? Yes, there is. I have
seen the impact of negative words on a child but I believe God's
word has the power to heal. It is not easy to overcome years of

negative input, but you can overcome by inputting the Word of God every single day. His words of comfort, promise and hope will day-by-day chip away at the words of man. God's Word will crowd negative thoughts out of your mind. As God's Word makes a positive impact, your angry thoughts and actions will become less and less. You can be the person you hoped to be as you take comfort and encouragement from His Word, His presence and His power in your life.

Jesus didn't respond to the crowd because He knew the best was yet to come. He knew that His Word was truth and He didn't need to argue the point with mocking people. It was hard to take the abuse on his human body as He cried, *"My God, My God why hast Thou forsaken me?* (v46)" But when He had taken the full brunt of our sin upon Himself, He yielded up His spirit (v50). He gave Himself for the purpose intended for His life on earth, and He yielded to His heavenly Father for His work in Heaven.

Jesus took the abuse so we wouldn't have to. And yet, if we do suffer abuse, He can help us follow His example of letting it go and moving forward by living a life delivered over to God. Expect God's encouragement and seek healing from His Word. Jesus cried out to Him, yielded to Him and will even forgive those who deliver the abuse and when they repent of their sin. "…Jesus was saying, *'Father, forgive them; for they do not know what they are doing."* Luke 23:34

Today's Prayer: *Lord Jesus, thank You for showing me how You reacted to mocking abuse. The abusive words I have heard in my life have impacted me in a negative way. I am praying today that you will diminish the negative in my life and fill me with the power of Your words of hope, encouragement and healing. Help me to forgive. Amen.*

G = Grief That Blames Others

"Now Martha said to Jesus, 'Lord if You had been here, my brother would not have died.'"
John 11:21

Scripture Reading: John 11:1-44

Actions that occur as a result of grief are expressed in different ways from different people. Such was the case with two sisters, Mary and Martha, when their brother died. These two sisters were so different in personality and interests, yet their grief was the same, but expressed with different emotion. Martha's grief was active, Mary's was passive. Martha had to be doing something to stay busy; Mary stayed at home and wept with sorrow.

Any person who suffers loss experiences grief. It is a natural part of the healing process and acceptance of the loss. But, everyone does not react in the same way. These sisters had sent for Jesus to save their brother days before he died, but Jesus was late in arriving. They didn't know that He had a purpose. When Martha heard He was almost there, she didn't wait for Him to arrive. She ran to meet Him and confronted Him saying, "If you had been here my brother would not have died." Was she angry? Were these angry words? We don't know the answer to that, but her action suggests she was aggressive and demanding. She didn't wait for Him to speak, but jumped right in with her accusatory statement. Mary's action upon seeing Jesus was to fall at His feet in sorrow. She spoke the same statement, but her grief was expressed in a very different way.

And then, even Jesus wept at the grave of their brother, his friend, Lazarus. Jesus knew grief. He grieved for the suffering of friends, and He grieved for the unbelief of the people around Him. His response to Martha was to assure her that her brother would rise again. He said *"I am the resurrection and the life. He who believes in Me, though he may die, he shall live. And whoever lives and believes in Me shall never die."* But then He asked her a question with four simple words, *"Do you believe this?"* Believing in a time of sorrow when we want to blame God is not easy, and yet, Martha said, *"Yes, Lord, I believe that You are the Christ, the Son of God, who is to come into the world."* It was that reminder of her faith that gave her comfort and peace to trust what He said.

Jesus responded to Martha's grief and possible anger:

- By meeting with her – v20

- By listening to her – v21

- By reassuring her – v23

- By reminding her of who He is and His power – v25

- By giving her an opportunity to respond by faith – v26-27

Grief causes different responses in us all. Some of us get angry and accuse others. Some of us weep in sorrow in the arms of others, but Jesus responds to us all in the same way with love, compassion and understanding. He has not left us alone in our grief even though it may seem like it at the time. He gives us all the opportunity to cling to our faith in order to walk the journey of grief toward hope and healing, trusting Him in the process. He asks the question of us all, "Do you believe this?" Do you believe He is the Resurrection and the Life? He who believes in Him shall live even if he dies. He is our hope in the midst of sorrow.

Today's Prayer: *Lord Jesus, thank You for knowing more about me than I know myself. Thank You for Your love and comfort in times of sorrow. Lord, I do believe. Amen*

Ɛ = Ɛnemy of the Soul

"...this man summoned Barnabas and Paul and sought to hear the word of God. But Elymas the magician was opposing them, seeking to turn the proconsul away from the faith."
Acts 13:7-8

Scripture Reading: Acts 13:1-12

The enemy of the soul will use whatever events and emotions we experience to drive us away from God. He wants us to be separated from the righteousness in God – that is his goal. The Devil will do what he can through his tricks and deceit to destroy our peace. If we are angry over circumstances in our lives, his goal is to feed the flame and keep us in that miserable state forever. When we allow the embers to become a roaring fire of anger in our hearts, it then becomes our own sin preventing us from hearing God speak to us with words of truth, forgiveness and healing.

In Acts 13, there was a man who wanted to hear the Word of God from Barnabas and Paul. But, a magician sought to turn the man away from faith through lies and fraud. However, Paul being filled with the Holy Spirit saw right through the ploys of the magician. He called him the son of the devil and enemy of all righteousness who was trying to make the straightway of the Lord crooked. Paul confronted the lies of the magician with God's truth.

Just as we have an enemy of the soul, we have an Advocate, one who is called alongside us to speak words of truth and protection over us. God used Paul to speak words of condemnation on the magician removing his power to trick with lies. As a result, the man who was seeking a word from God not only received it, but witnessed God's power and protection, and he believed. *"Then the proconsul believed when he saw what had happened, being amazed at the teaching of the Lord."* (Acts 13:12)

If your heart and mind are filled with lies that are feeding your anger, you will not be able to get beyond the anger until you confront the lies with truth.

- No one cares…

- No one understands what happened to me…

- If God cared, He would not let this happen…

- I can't go on without _____…

Thoughts like these are all lies planted in your heart by the enemy of the soul who wants to separate you from the love and righteousness of God. Confront the lies with truth! You have an Advocate, Jesus Christ the righteous, who intercedes for you with the Father. He came to destroy the words of the devil (I John 3:8). The lies that are attempting to destroy your peace can be confronted and overcome through Him. Tell Him your struggles, your fears, your angry thoughts. Ask Him to destroy the power of the lies with His power of truth.

Today's Prayer: *Lord Jesus, lies have landed upon the logs of my anger turning it into a raging fire. Please replace these lies with Your truth that I may be reconciled with God and no longer tempted to lash out because of circumstances fueled by negative thinking. Forgive me for falling into the trap of the enemy of my soul. Thank You for being my Advocate. Amen.*

R = Rejection Hurts

"And coming to Him as to a living stone, rejected by men, but choice and precious in the sight of God..."
First Peter 2:4

Rejection is painful. It hurts to be turned away from someone you like or love, no matter the reason. Rejection indicates a disapproval of some kind that casts off that which is examined and found lacking. And just like the other negative emotions discussed in the anger acrostic devotionals, the pain of rejection can cause anger. Even Jesus was rejected, but that didn't stop Him from living out His earthly purpose for eternal glory. *"Jesus said to them, 'The stone which the builders rejected, this became the chief corner stone; this came about from the Lord, and it is marvelous in our eyes'."* (Matthew 21:42)

When rejected by friends or loved ones, try to press on toward your earthly purpose with a Heavenly goal. Keep your eyes focused on those things above rather than dwelling on the rejection until you begin to fume and resent those who rejected you. Choose to move toward those that do accept you for who you are. When Jesus was rejected by His own people, He went to those who accepted Him as God's Son. They believed and benefited while those who rejected Him were shamed and proven wrong.

Rather than live with the pain of rejection, choose the path of acceptance. Follow Jesus. He loves you as you are. God does not reject those who seek Him with their whole heart. He will meet you at your point of need and take you just as you are. Ask Him to fill your heart with His love to the point of squeezing out all resentment and anger toward those who have hurt you.

Today's Prayer: *Lord, thank You for accepting me as I am flaws and all. As I seek You today, I ask that You will replace the anger and resentment in my heart with Your love so that nothing will hinder my purpose on earth from being accomplished for Your glory. Forgive those who have hurt me, and help me to forgive as well. In Jesus Name, Amen.*

Section Two

Quenching Flames – Turning Anger Around

~~Negative Impact~~	Focused On the Positive
A	Acceptance and Adjustments in Life
N	New Way of Life
G	Grace Abundant and Free
E	Encouragement for the Soul
R	Redemptive Relationship

$\mathcal{A}$ = $\mathcal{A}$cceptance and $\mathcal{A}$djustments in $\mathcal{L}$ife

"Cast your burden upon the LORD, and He will sustain you; He will never allow the righteous to be shaken."
Psalm 55:22

Scripture Reading: Psalm 55

When loss occurs, suddenly things are different. Our heart longs for everything to be the same as it was yesterday, but our mind knows the reality of what now is. Many emotions are at odds with one another confusing our mental and emotional system. In order to begin to heal, there must come a time of acceptance of what is now the new reality. At this point, adjustments to the changes in your life will begin to take place.

When the Psalmist stated that the one causing him anguish was his companion and familiar friend, this was his moment of acceptance to the new reality in his life. The reality was that he had lost forever his friend. That relationship was gone. Things would not be the same again.

Is there someone you loved but have lost? Has the loss caused you such anguish that anger is controlling your emotions? The Psalmist accepted the loss, but something else needed to occur and that is adjustment.

Any time there is loss, change will occur. And change necessitates adjustment! The Psalmist acknowledged, accepted and adjusted by giving his burden to God and trusting Him to help him cope with the new reality of his life.

Be encouraged that the loss is not the end of you. It is the beginning of something different, and you can accept and adjust with God's help. He will carry your burden of pain and anguish. Give it to Him and trust Him to carry you through the acceptance and adjustment of loss toward healing and a new tomorrow.

Today's Prayer: *Lord, I cast my burden upon You knowing You care for me. I pray for Your strength and healing in my heart and mind. Thank You for the knowledge that You are here now and will be in all my tomorrows no matter what changes occur in my life. Help me to accept and adjust to them according to Your will. Amen.*

$\mathcal{N}$ = $\mathcal{N}$ew Way of Life

"Therefore we have been buried with Him through baptism into death, in order that as Christ was raised from the dead through the glory of the Father, so we too might walk in newness of life."
Romans 6:4

Scripture Reading: Romans 6:4-7

Addressing the issue of negative emotions in your life is hard work! They don't just go away simply because you want them to. However, wanting them to go away is a step in the right direction. The next step is to identify them and examine the source. Why am I angry? What is causing my negative reaction? Once the source has been identified, you then have a choice. Do I continue to be aggressive toward others with my words and actions, or do I take the high road? Isaiah 35:8-10 describes the highway of the redeemed, the road they travel as God's chosen. There will be no fools or danger on this highway. There will be no sorrow there, only gladness and joy. The ransomed of the Lord will walk on it. It is high and it is holy. Take the high road by walking in the newness of life you have through Christ. Lay aside the old way when angry words cause pain. Allow the love of God to fill your heart through Christ Jesus.

The next step is where the work really begins; that is the persistent, daily, and often moment-by-moment prayer. We cannot change by ourselves but only as we yield our emotions and lives to Christ are we able to change. If you are in Christ, you are a new creation. The old you is no longer, but a new you has been born. *"For if we have become united with Him in the likeness of His death, certainly we shall be also in the likeness of His resurrection, knowing this, that our old self was crucified with Him, that our body of sin might be done away with, that we should no longer be slaves to sin; for he who has died is freed from sin."* (Romans 6:5-7)

Take advantage of the new you in Christ to walk in the newness of life available to you by applying the following:

- Decide you want to change.

- Identify and examine the source of negative emotions.

- Choose to respond with hope and encouragement rather than reacting in anger. 4. Persistently pray to address your need.

- Accept that you are a new creation in Christ and live accordingly. *"Therefore if any man is in Christ, he is a new creature; the old things passed away; behold, new things have come."* Second Corinthians 5:17

Today's Prayer: *Jesus, thank You for making it possible for the old me to die and the new me to be born in You. Help me to live according to the new creation that I have become from accepting You as my Savior. Amen*

G = Grace Abundant and Free

"For by grace you have been saved through faith;
and that not of yourselves, it is the gift of God; not
as a result of works, that no one should boast."
Ephesians 2:8-9

Scripture Reading: Second Corinthians 12:7-10;
Titus 3:4-7

There has been a lot of speculation through the years about what the Apostle Paul was speaking of when he said he had been given a "thorn in the flesh". The fact that the thorn is not identified leaves room for personal application of whatever our own source of irritation may be. But the most freeing statement from these verses comes from Jesus to Paul when He said, *"My grace is sufficient for you, for power is perfected in weakness"* (Second Corinthians 12:9).

Paul talked about thorns and weakness. Jesus answered with grace and power. Grace in this verse is the divine influence upon the heart and it's reflection in a life. This grace is a gift bringing joy and pleasure. Jesus was saying to Paul, my divine influence upon your heart is sufficient for you to overcome the irritations of life in order to experience joy. The power of Jesus is greater than the weaknesses of man.

It is the gift of God's grace that saves us from sin according to Romans 5:21 and Titus 3:4-7. It is this same grace that is applied in our failures and weaknesses. And it is by God's grace that we are able to overcome negative emotions when we take them to the throne of grace and leave them there. Scripture tells us that we find grace and receive mercy to help us in our time of need when we draw near with confidence to the throne of grace (Hebrews 4:16). Drawing near with confidence is to go to God believing that He will help you when you are struggling. What a privilege to be given the hope of God's grace.

Today's Prayer: *Gracious Heavenly Father, thank You that Your grace is sufficient to provide what I need to cope with those areas of my life that I cannot change. But even more wonderful is the privilege of drawing near to Your throne of grace to leave my burdens there for receiving help in time of need. I praise You for Your mercy and saving grace. In Jesus Name, Amen.*

ℰ = Encouragement for the Soul

"In the same way God, desiring even more to show to the heirs of the promise the unchangeableness of His purpose, interposed with an oath, in order that by two unchangeable things, in which it is impossible for God to lie, we may have strong encouragement, we who have fled for refuge in laying hold of the hope set before us."
Hebrews 6:17-18

Scripture Reading: Hebrews 6

We all need encouragement! Unfortunately, many individuals are dragged down by the discouragement of words, actions or circumstances that make a negative impact upon their lives. Living with this kind of discouragement over a period of time creates a smoldering fire of anger and resentment within that keeps us from being able to enjoy the peace and joy of God's intention for us.

The enemy discourages with lies, but our Advocate encourages with truth. In the Bible Dictionary, the same Greek word is used for "advocate" and "encouragement". Therefore, Jesus is not only our Advocate alongside us for protection, but also our source of hope filling us with encouragement. Be encouraged today with the hope we have as an anchor of the soul, a hope both sure and steadfast. As you read the verses in Hebrews 6, you see several important facts:

- It is impossible for God to lie.

- He gives encouragement by two unchangeable things – His promise and His oath.

- This encouragement comes as we flee to the refuge of hope He has set before us.

I find great comfort in knowing that when tempted to believe the lies of the enemy, God does not lie. I can turn to His Word for truth. When tempted to be discouraged by things beyond my control, God encourages through His promise of eternal life and His oath of truth and commitment. And what a tremendous encouragement it is to know that I can flee to the refuge of hope He has given in Christ Jesus who is steadfast, always dependable and the same yesterday, today and forever! He is my encouragement and I will hope in Him.

Today's Prayer: *Father, thank You for the hope and encouragement You gave us in Your promise of eternal life through Jesus – a promise that will never change. Thank You that He is my refuge and I can run to Him with all my discouragements knowing He is my hope. Amen.*

R = Redemptive Relationship

"...knowing that you were not redeemed with perishable things like silver or gold from your futile way of life inherited from your forefathers, but with precious blood, as of the lamb unblemished and spotless, the blood of Christ."
First Peter 1:18-19

Scripture Reading: Book of Ruth

What is a redemptive relationship? You may think, "Well, it is one that encourages, it is good and positive, a healthy relationship." Yes, it may be all of those things. However, a redemptive relationship is only made necessary through suffering, loss or separation from God by sin. And, it is not accomplished without a price being paid to buy back that which was lost and separated.

In the Old Testament book of Ruth, Naomi suffered the loss of her husband and sons, one of which was the husband of Ruth. In order to survive, she had to sell the land belonging to her husband – his inheritance. In order to redeem the inheritance of her family, a price was paid by a relative to buy back the land and marry the widow Ruth. There was suffering, grief, loss, and separation requiring redemption. Someone had to be willing to pay the price of redemption, and it was done. There was a cost involved for Boaz, the kinsman redeemer, but he was willing and able to pay. The inheritance was redeemed. (Ruth 4:4-10)

Many have suffered the loss of loved ones and have been forced to sell property in order to survive. The property is lost to them forever unless someone is willing to buy it back for them. Most of the time that does not happen in today's world. Relatives are no longer willing and/or able to take on the responsibilities of their deceased brother's family and property. Things have changed to the point that everyone struggles to survive whether married or not. Each family unit has their own problems and financial struggles to deal with. We all need a Redeemer!

What we do have today and forever is the hope of a redemptive relationship for those who do not know Christ, and for those who believe in Him, we have that hope within us. We have been redeemed! The separation is a result of sin and the suffering is a result of the undesirable condition of separation from God. But the most important part of this equation is the reality of the price paid for redemption from sin. That is the blood of an unblemished lamb – Jesus Christ! He paid the penalty for our sin so we would not have to. He is our Redeemer!

And no, that does not mean our personal property is restored or our deceased loved one is returned to us. What it means is that our eternal soul has been purchased back from the destruction of sin and eternal death. Our peace on earth is in knowing that we will forever be with the Lord in eternity. Our promise is that of no more tears, no more night, but rather, to live in the eternal joy and light of our Living Savior – our Redeemer, the LORD Jesus Christ.

This redemptive relationship is what gives comfort in loss and grief as well as love and grace in times of human rejection. Our Redeemer is strong and mighty to save. Our property on earth may not be restored, but our Redeemer has a mansion in Heaven reserved for us!

Today's Prayer: *Lord, thank You for buying me back from the destruction of my soul and for paying the penalty for my sins with Your blood. Forgive me for those times when I have been discouraged by suffering and rejection, and thank You for being a constant source of hope, love and encouragement in my life. Amen.*

Section Two

Quenching Flames –
Moving Beyond Anger

You Can Quench the Flames of Anger

"Do not quench the Spirit..."
First Thessalonians 5:19

*"And do not grieve the Holy Spirit of God, by whom
you were sealed for the day of redemption."*
Ephesians 4:30

Scripture Reading: Ephesians 4:30-32

We can *quench* the Holy Spirit of God in our lives by not responding to Him and the work He desires to do through us. We can also *grieve* the Holy Spirit by doing those things that are sin. But, the good news is that we can reverse this by allowing the Holy Spirit to quench the flames of anger in our hearts so as not to cause grief but to exhibit peace and joy. However, this can only be accomplished by having a redemptive relationship with Christ our Redeemer.

Anger is a negative and undesirable condition. It holds us captive in its grip. But redemption is the release from an undesirable condition having been bought with a price. In Jeremiah 50:34, Israel was held captive and the captors refused to let them go. But the Scripture says, their Redeemer is strong. It was their Redeemer who released them from captivity.

In order to be redeemed from the undesirable condition of sin, a price was paid to buy us back – the blood of Christ. If you are in Christ, you have a redemptive relationship. You have the ability within you to quench the flames of anger that are making you miserable.

Does this mean that if I am angry all the time that I am not a Christian? No, that is not what it means. Anger that is righteous and dealt with in a righteous way is not sin. Anger becomes sin when it is allowed to fester and grow into bitterness and an unforgiving heart that interrupts your fellowship with God and quenches His Spirit.

When the hole left in your life by grief and loss is filled with anger, the Spirit is quenched. However, as a Christian, you have the power of the Holy Spirit within you to throw cold water all over the flames of anger, quenching the anger rather than the Spirit. The power is in grace and forgiveness of the Holy Spirit, both for you and through you toward whatever is the root of the anger. It is not easy, but it is well worth the work involved to force out the anger by ripping out the root, therefore, making room for the Holy Spirit to fill the empty hole. It is only as you deal with the cause and pull out the root that your relationships will be whole again, both with God and with others. How can this be accomplished? The answer lies in peace and forgiveness.

"See to it that no one comes short of the grace of God; that no root of bitterness springing up causes trouble, and by it many be defiled..." (Hebrews 12:15). Those three words 'see to it' mean to look at the 'it' as your responsibility to act. The responsibility in this verse is to not fall short of God's grace. That is accomplished by eliminating every possibility of bitterness in order to avoid trouble. Look at the following Scriptures for guidance.

"Pursue peace with all men, and the sanctification without which no one will see the Lord." (Hebrews 12:14). Look for ways to be at peace with others.

"For He delivered us from the domain of darkness, and transferred us to the kingdom of His beloved Son in whom we have redemption, the forgiveness of sins." (Colossians 1:13-14)

"And be kind to one another, tender-hearted, forgiving each other, just as God in Christ also has forgiven you." (Ephesians 4:32.) Have you forgiven those who have treated you unjustly? God says to forgive them. We will not have peace or completely get rid of the anger unless we are willing to forgive.

We have been redeemed so that we may have peace. How can we do any less than practice the same forgiveness that was accomplished for us through the redemptive relationship we have in Christ?

Today's Prayer: *Father, forgive my unforgiving heart. Help me to forgive _____ for I am willing Lord. Fill me with Your grace that I may extend it to others. Amen.*

Fatigue Fuels the Flame

"You, who seek God, let your heart revive.
For the Lord hears the needy..."
Psalm 69:32b-33a

Scripture Reading: Psalm 69

We live in a fast-paced world filled with more activity than any one person was intended to be part of. And yet, we keep doing, doing, doing without giving our minds and bodies time to rest. Add to an already overactive mind and body the emotional upheaval of a crisis, and that means trouble. A mind that is fractured by stress and trauma, plus a body exhausted, is an emotional crisis. This kind of fatigue fuels the flame for an angry outburst. Angry outbursts are costly. They cost relationships, respect, integrity and our witness for Christ.

And so, what is the solution for this kind of fatigue. Psalm 69 is a prayer to God in which the Psalmist describes his physical and emotional state as well as his spiritual need. In verses two and three, he relates his failing physical strength and feels he is stuck in quicksand with no foothold while he drowns from deep waters flooding over him. In verse three, he describes his emotional state of mind. He has cried to the point of being completely dried out. Can you relate to these feelings of hopelessness and helplessness from an exhaustion that has left you dry?

The rest of the prayer is stating all of the details of his condition and circumstance to the Lord with a cry for redemption and deliverance. *"Deliver me from the mire, and do not let me sink..."*

(Verse 14). Do not let me sink. Have you been so exhausted at times that you felt as if you were sinking and could not pull yourself back up again? When the body and mind have gone long periods of time without rest from activity and/or difficulty, burnout happens. It is time to rest in the Lord. *"Answer me, O LORD, for Thy loving kindness is good; according to the greatness of Thy compassion, turn to me..."* (Verse 16)

When activity and stress are overwhelming your life, follow the pattern of the Psalmist prayer. Go to God admitting your human frailties. Tell Him what you are feeling and the circumstances that have dragged you down. Ask for deliverance and to be lifted high out of the state you are in. And then, most important of all, praise the name of God with song. (Verse 30) I know that when I am exhausted, nothing picks me up better than to listen to praise songs about the goodness of God and to sing along with those songs. Keeping worship songs on CD in your vehicle for just such a time is a great antidote to negative emotions and fatigue. Keep your radio dial on a Christian music station so it comes on automatically when you turn the ignition key.

Singing praise to God is not only refreshing, but fills your heart with peace that prevents anger from rising to the surface. *"...The God of Israel Himself gives strength and power to the people. Blessed be God!"* (Psalm 68:35b)

Today's Prayer: *O LORD, how majestic is Your name in all the earth. You are mighty to be praised. Revive my heart and body to lift me from the miry clay of exhaustion that I may once again serve You with passion and joy. Amen.*

When Crisis Interrupts...Power Intervenes

"Now may the God of peace Himself sanctify you entirely; and may your spirit and soul and body be preserved complete, without blame at the coming of our Lord Jesus Christ."
First Thessalonians 5:23

Scripture Reading: Romans 8:26-39

During the writing and compiling of this devotional series, we learned that my husband's cancer had returned. At the halfway mark of his radiation treatment he was weak and, therefore, frustrated at being slowed down from the work he loves. At one point, I detected anger in his words and attitude. We talked about it and were reminded that anger is a very real human emotion that occurs when we have to accept the fact that we have absolutely no control over a crisis like this in life. It is similar to that of a victim who has suffered violence against them from a perpetrator. They had no control of the actions against them. As we talked, we began to apply the principals from God's word to our own lives that we try to help other wounded people understand.

- We simply cannot endure the crisis without the power of the Holy Spirit in our lives. Anger quenches the Spirit and interrupts our line of communication with God and others. In order to restore healthy relationships, anger must be dealt with and eliminated, if we are to experience the power of God to heal. (I Thessalonians 5:23.)

- We are dependent upon the intercessory prayers of others, but especially the intercession of the Holy Spirit on our behalf (Romans 8:26).

- It is only by God's strength that we are able to travel this journey of life, for in our weakness, He is made strong (Second Corinthians 12:9-10).

- Anger toward aging, illness and crisis may be a normal human reaction, but it certainly does not benefit the process of healing the body. One of the most frustrating things about cancer is that there is no one toward whom you can direct your anger! And so, the anger pours out on whoever may be around at the moment. If you are trying to go on about business as usual, others may have an expectation that you are able to carry on as usual. If that is the case, others will not understand that an angry response *with* them is not really *toward* them! So, it is important to know your limitations and retreat to the best of your ability for a while as your body recovers and heals. Rest in the Lord. His grace is sufficient for you. God's Word tells us that He is our refuge and strength, a very present help in trouble, and to *"cease striving and know that I am God"*. (Psalm 46:1,10; Psalm 37:7-8; II Corinthians 12:9)

- We have learned that when an angry retort has damaged a relationship, God wants us to seek forgiveness, (Second Corinthians 2:10; Matthew 6:14-15) and to humble ourselves before God and anyone we may have offended in our anger. Our God is a forgiving God (First John 1:9). He knows the heart of man. He knows the crisis of the moment. And we know that in order to have peace in our hearts, we must ask Him to cleanse our hearts of all unrighteousness, including anger (Psalm 51:10).

Jesus is our Peace. Therefore, we know the anger of the moment can be replaced by His forgiving love (Ephesians 2:14). This same forgiving love is available to anyone! If you are in crisis due to health, loss or trauma, Jesus is your peace. Call upon His Holy Name (Romans 9:9), seek His forgiveness, the forgiveness of others (Ephesians 4:32), and you will be filled with a peace that is beyond human understanding (Philippians 4:7).

Today's Prayer: *Heavenly Father, we are so humbled by the power of your Holy Spirit, which reminds us of our sin and shows the way to forgiveness. Forgive us for trying to put our crisis into the category of a human solution by becoming angry when there is no one to blame. We acknowledge that we are totally dependent upon you and no matter the outcome of the crisis we know we are safe in your loving arms. Help us to rest in you more knowing that you will provide for our every need. Forgive us our sins as we have forgiven those who have sinned against us, and help others to do the same. In Jesus name, Amen.*

Drawn to the Well

"Then God opened her eyes and she saw a well of water. And she went and filled the skin with water and gave the lad a drink."
Genesis 21:19

Scripture Reading: John 4:1-45

While writing, I am sitting in the backyard of my daughter and son-in-law's home in Houston, Texas in the middle of July. It is quiet in the early morning hours as I study, but it is hot! Even though Houston is not a desert, the temperature can soar well into the hundreds. There is an oasis in this yard; a beautiful pool of water with palm trees and foliage surrounding it.

Sitting here in the heat, the coolness of the refreshing water is calling to me. I am drawn to it. It refreshes my spirit just to see the ripples and hear the music made by the fall of water from the fountain.

And so, in studying from the book of Genesis, it is easy to understand why we often find God's people resting by a well. They, too, were drawn to the water for a time of rest and refreshment. For example, in Genesis 24:11, Abraham's servant went to a well and it is there he met Isaac's wife. In Genesis 29:2, Jacob met and fell in love with Rachel at a well.

Throughout Scripture, we find important things happening at the place where water exists. God provides these wells or "oasis" in the desert as a gathering place for making His provisions known to His people and for giving hope. When Abraham sent Hagar into the desert with her son Ishmael, God provided a well of water for her in the middle of her desert experience and at the point of her desperation. Genesis 21:19 says that *"God opened her eyes and she saw a well of water."* God provided a miracle in the life of a woman in the desert who was dry, thirsty and without hope.

Are you in a desert time of your life feeling dry and thirsty? Have you been taken from a place of prosperity to a place of desolation? Have you been forced out of your comfort zone by circumstances beyond your control? Take heart in knowing that your sorrow is but a moment and joy cometh in the morning.

When you look at Jeremiah 31, you find a verse tucked in the middle stating God's promise to refresh those who sorrow and satisfy those who are weary. And even as I am writing these words, a cool gentle breeze has stirred over the water on this hot July day in Houston. God does satisfy in the heat of the moment. He does provide refreshment for a dry and weary soul.

God satisfies with Living Water that the world cannot provide. John 4:1-45 talks about the Living Water God has provided to satisfy your weary soul and dry spirit. In this passage of Scripture we once again see a Man at a well. And once again we see a woman drawn to the well with conversation between the two. The Man was Jesus. It is in this passage that we see the first introduction of "Living Water" as Jesus identified Himself to the woman at the well.

She was a woman who needed the Living Water of forgiveness from the oasis that only Jesus can provide. You will never know true joy apart from the Living Water that springs up to eternal life. This is the point Jesus was making to her. He is the Living Water, the only oasis for our hearts that will fully satisfy those who sorrow. And with this satisfaction in the midst of our desert experiences, joy springs forth.

As you look back to the examples from Genesis on the meetings at the wells, you find men who were placed there to be used by God in the lives of individual women at that specific time and for His purpose. God drew women to the well for a purpose He revealed at that place of refreshment, a purpose that would impact the men and women involved.

God is still drawing people to the well of "Living Water" today. He draws us from our desert experiences of rejection, loneliness, sorrow, pain, anger, illness, sin or whatever it is that depletes your supply of strength and joy. He refreshes the weary soul just simply with His presence. In those desert times, we don't have to give in to our emotions leading to anger, depression and despair. You can press through those negative emotions trusting God.

Just as the pool in front of me is drawing me to enter, Jesus draws us to Him. And in Him, our very own oasis, we are made whole and delivered from the desert. But it is through our desert experiences that we learn to press on to follow Him as we grow in our faith. Be strengthened in your trust and faith of the only One who makes the provision needed in your desert experience, and allow yourself to be drawn to the well of life.

Today's Prayer: *Father, thank You for your presence in my desert. Thank You for the cool breeze of Your spirit who draws me to Living Water and refreshes my soul. Help me to partake of Your refreshment. Amen*

Going Without Knowing

"...I will bless you..."
Genesis 12:1b

There was once a man in the Old Testament days of the Bible who had lived in the same place all his life until.....

The Bible tells us that *"the Lord said to Abram, 'Leave your country, your people and your father's household and go to the land I will show you'"*, and so Abram left as the Lord had told him to do. He was seventy five years old. He was asked to go to a place he had never been, but he did so trusting in the wisdom of God.

Was it easy to leave his homeland behind and the people he had known all his life? No, he had many hardships along the way. But with those difficulties came the blessings of God as He provided and protected Abram as He led him to a land He promised. Abram went with trust and confidence that no matter what happened, God would be with him, and God would bless him because He promised He would.

I'm sure Abram (whose name was later changed to Abraham) had many questions, but he went anyway, trusting God for the answers to be revealed when the time was right. I'm sure you have many questions right now in a situation that is very difficult to understand, and even though there are not answers in this moment, there is direction. The direction for you is the same as it was for Abraham long, long ago – that direction is simply to do the next thing.

Abraham didn't know where he was going or how long he would be there, but when he was told to go, he did the next thing. He packed up and made himself ready for the journey. All along the way he didn't know what tomorrow would bring, but he did the next thing that would carry him further into the journey. When trouble blocked his way, he did the next thing and listened to direction from God.

As you travel your journey of grief without knowing what the future holds, it can be frustrating and emotionally draining. But God directs us to do the next thing, and that can mean letting go of what is holding us back - letting go of negative emotions that are damaging. You can do it with God's help. The Bible tells us that His Word is a lamp unto our feet (Psalm 119:105) lighting the path before us. Without a doubt, we can trust His direction when things are uncertain.

In this journey you have been taken through anger and its causes, hopefully you have learned to turn to God for help and are ready to move to the next phase of recovery from your emotional turmoil caused by grief. God will always guide us to do the next thing. I can't wait to see where the journey with Him leads. He promises satisfaction and refreshing that does not fail.

> *"And the LORD will continually guide you, and satisfy your desire in scorched places, and give strength to your bones; And you will be like a watered garden, And like a spring of water whose waters do not fail."*
> Isaiah 58:11

Do you know Him? If there has not been a time in your life when you have accepted Jesus Christ as your Lord and Savior, pray this simple prayer.

Today's Prayer: *Jesus I need You in my life. Today I acknowledge that my life is not what it needs to be because of the sin that has kept me from You. I ask that You come into my life as my Savior to forgive my sin and direct me in the next thing, whatever it may be. Thank You for loving me. Amen.*